42
COMMANDO
ROYAL MARINES
IN THE FALKLANDS WAR

42 COMMANDO ROYAL MARINES
IN THE FALKLANDS WAR

A STORY OF GOOD EGGS AND DODGY OPPOS

The Unreliable Memoirs of a 1980s
Royal Marine Commando.
Almost in action!

MARK LEWIS

Pen & Sword
MILITARY

AN IMPRINT OF PEN & SWORD BOOKS LTD.
YORKSHIRE - PHILADELPHIA

First published in Great Britain in 2025 by
PEN AND SWORD MILITARY
An imprint of
Pen & Sword Books Limited
Yorkshire – Philadelphia

ISBN 978 1 03613 246 0

Typeset in Times New Roman 11.5/14.5 by
SJmagic DESIGN SERVICES, India.
Printed and bound in the UK by CPI Group (UK) Ltd.

The Publisher's authorised representative in the EU for product safety is
Authorised Rep Compliance Ltd., Ground Floor, 71 Lower Baggot Street,
Dublin D02 P593, Ireland.
www.arccompliance.com

For a complete list of Pen & Sword titles please contact
PEN & SWORD BOOKS LIMITED
George House, Units 12 & 13, Beevor Street, Off Pontefract Road,
Barnsley, South Yorkshire, S71 1HN, England
E-mail: enquiries@pen-and-sword.co.uk
Website: www.pen-and-sword.co.uk

or

PEN AND SWORD BOOKS
1950 Lawrence Rd, Havertown, PA 19083, USA
E-mail: uspen-and-sword@casematepublishers.com
Website: www.penandswordbooks.com

CONTENTS

PROLOGUE: MARCH 1979 – YOMPING ON

I felt the unrelenting winter rain of Dartmoor, being driven by the icy Atlantic wind, blow into the gap between my ill-fitting boots and puttees.[1] However, painful blisters agitated by thin woollen issue socks saturated with freezing water was no excuse to slacken the pace.

Aching cold muscles cramped as we yomped[2] on through the darkness. A backbreaking unwieldy large pack, attached to stiff frozen webbing, rubbed against every bony part of my waist and shoulders. My knees threatened to give way with each step that I took through the freezing bog. My legs were covered in runny, cold, black peat that then clung to my sodden trousers.

Hands numb from the wrists down did their best to maintain the hold of the SLR Rifle in the alert position.

No rifle strap to make it easier to carry.

No gloves to give even the slightest reprieve from the biting cold.

'The weapon is always carried at the alert in the field, so a strap is pointless,' the troop officer informed us at the start of training. 'Gloves are only for when it's really cold.'

My empty stomach was gnawing for an energy-giving Mars Bar, but that was deep in the side pouch of my large pack and completely unobtainable while on the move.

Gusting horizontal rain whipped sweat sideways from my face before it even had the chance to form a drip from my nose.

---

1. Puttees: A covering of the lower part of the leg from the ankle to the knee.
2. Yomp: To march over difficult terrain with heavy equipment.

My heavy woollen 'noddy cap'[3] wobbled on my head with each jarring step. If I finish this exercise, I thought, I would be one step closer to transforming it into a mythical Green Beret!

We had been yomping for days on this exercise, and we were going to yomp all night with little chance of any sleep until ENDEX (End of Exercise) was called at some unknown – and therefore almost irrelevant – time later that week.

Too many exercises were unexpectedly extended, and too many transport RZ (rendezvous) points had been navigated to, only to have the 4-tonner drivers being told to drive off as we were informed, with glee, by the training team that we were yomping back.

You only fall for that once!

From that point on, you only believe them when you actually arrive back at Commando Training Centre Royal Marines and the 4-tonne trucks drive through the elevated main gate barrier with you in the back. It's all in the head. Don't give up. It had gotten to a point where I didn't think they could make it any more difficult, and I was still hacking it. 'I can do this!' But why on earth did I want to?

---

3. A Noddy Cap is a woollen cap issued to Royal Marine recruits when they start the last four weeks and the 'Commando Tests' phase of training. The top of these caps tended to 'flip out' and wave about when the recruit was running, similar to the character Noddy's blue cap.

FEBRUARY 1977

M y Dad had just died in front of me. He was 49, and my family were devastated. I was a 14-year-old boy who had just lost his role model and hero, and I didn't have a clue what to do.

Dad had been a Royal Marine for twenty-two years. He was part of the war generation, and had been to pretty much every post-war conflict from Palestine in 1948 to Aden in 1968. He was so fit and able to do everything – from using his engineering skills to build extensions on our house to fixing bikes and making basic Marine ration-style dinners that we all ate when required; although we still looked forward to Mum's slightly better-presented family meals when Dad was busy at work.

The Royal Marines had made him an all-round decent, well-balanced family man who was proud of his past. But he was looking forward to his future, having spent the last ten years training and working as a very successful social worker. He had a talent for turning his hand to anything and doing it well.

After his death, I spent the next eighteen months at school in a trance.

My mother was hugely supportive and strong, but in shock. My clever brother, who was a year older than me and at grammar school, lost his focus and gained very poor results for one so bright. My loving sister, who was working in the hotel industry, had left home and we could not support her, nor have her support us. My lovely family unit was adrift, without a rudder.

I felt dreadfully unsupported by teachers at school, who either pretended that all was fine or ignored me in the hope that I wouldn't break down in front of them and cause them to have to show some emotion. I didn't break down; I just held it in. However, one teacher did stand out. Mr Rainy, also an ex-war Royal Marine who knew exactly

1

how to keep an eye on me and demonstrated great kindness at that most difficult time in my life.

So, what was I to do? In conversations with my Dad, I had mentioned joining the Royal Marines, but he had unequivocally put me off the idea and become quite animated with other career options, recommending becoming a carpenter or better still joining the police force. Anything other than joining the Royal Marines.

When I was about to leave school, I had the compulsory meeting with the unimaginative careers officer who, unlike my Dad, seemed to have very little foresight. When I stated that I'd thought about joining the Royal Marines, he agreed instantly and ended the interview.

It wasn't a difficult decision to make; at least not for me.

I had heard all about my Dad's life as a Colour Sergeant in the Royal Marines. I had seen all the photos of Dad on active service with his mates, all lined up grinning at the camera with various weapons and captured enemy kit displayed – in desert kit, in jungle kit, in smart No.1 uniform.

Our family life growing up in Plymouth had been full of happy adventures: camping, going on wildlife walks, rafting, sailing and swimming.

As a child, I had visited Stonehouse Barracks in Plymouth with him many times, and had observed him and his mates just enjoying each other's company and having a laugh. Royal Marines seemed to instantly start clowning around when someone's child was brought into the barracks. My brother and I would invariably go home with gifts of cakes or some inert weaponry that would make us the obvious leaders in the next woodland expedition with our mates, but would also make Mum frown and ask awkward questions to my Dad about why we needed yet another large metal military object in the back garden.

What tipped the decision for me, though, was a burning desire to find out what my Dad had gone through and to experience some of his adventures.

So, I applied!

WE WILL LOOK AFTER YOU

I walked into the Royal Navy and Royal Marines recruiting office at 15 years of age whilst still attending school. I weighed 10 stone and was very fresh-faced at 5ft 7in tall. The Royal Navy Chief Petty Officer smiled as I approached the Royal Marines Colour Sergeant sitting at the desk next to him. Was he being friendly to a potential rating, or did he just think I was an interested school child collecting leaflets for some school project?

The Colour Sergeant eyed me up and down when I explained to him that I wanted to join the Royal Marines. He politely explained the process of joining up, but it seemed like he was just going through the motions. Like he didn't really think I had what it takes. Some other potential naval recruits and I then took a test, which the Colour Sergeant reluctantly informed me that I had passed.

'Suppose I should interview you then,' he said.

There then followed the usual questions: Why did I want to join? What skills could I offer? Etc., etc. When he got to my Father's occupation, I informed him that he had died of a heart attack 18 months ago, but that he used to be a Colour Sergeant in 45 Commando Royal Marines, and this was one of the reasons I had picked the Marines. With this, the recruiting sergeant put down his pen and asked me a few confirming questions about my Dad's twenty-two-year career.

He then said, 'Well, if we can't look after one of our own, who can we look after? When do you leave school?'

Three weeks after my sixteenth birthday, I stepped off the train at Commando Training Centre Royal Marines, Lympstone. I was now, 5ft 7½in tall and weighed 10½ stone.

Judging by the reception that the corporals gave me, I felt that I would need to use the 'Dad was in the Corp for twenty-two years' line on them as well, but they were all too busy shouting at us to listen, and I was too busy running with all my bags and all the other fresh-faced recruits in a sort of three-rank, out-of-step melee.

The corporals seemed delighted when some unfortunate recruit's suitcase burst open, scattering the contents up the steps leading away from the railway station. They set about him like hunting dogs around a kill; all keen to regurgitate favourite insults and terms of abuse for just such an occasion. Even if one of the training team was interested in my Dad's part in Britain's post-war withdrawal from the Empire, they wouldn't have heard it because of all the shouting that their colleagues were doing. Corps history would no doubt be covered in some lectures later on in training, but for now, we would just stick to the running whilst they did the shouting.

Just before I joined, I had taken a temporary job for three months, working as a plumber's mate on some building sites, and the swearing-in that all-male environment had been a bit of a shock after leaving school. I recognized that I had the same, although heightened, feeling of shock here. The corporals used even more advanced swear words, which were crafted into verbs and adjectives to 'instruct and encourage' us to move between the accommodation blocks towards the waiting area. Here, the training team could scrutinize us even more closely and start to make unsupportive comments on potential junior marines' haircuts and attire. 'More fucking hair on you than a badger's bum!' 'Does your Grandad know that you've stolen his demob suit?'

The notice in the joining instructions stated that the 'Welcome Meeting' was the next item on the agenda. Maybe the corporals didn't get a copy.

TRAINING AND MAP SKILLS

There was a certain amount of what today would be described as 'bullying' going on at Commando Training Centre Royal Marines (CTCRM), Lympstone, in 1978. My experience was that it was mainly recruit on recruit, but the training teams kept us all so busy that this soon fizzled out as there was no energy left to prat about.

The kick-out and opt-out rate of us 'nods'[4] was staggering! We started with sixty on the first day, and in the first few weeks people would disappear on a daily basis. The training teams seemed to hold all power over who would go and who would stay. In their eyes, anyone who left was a 'wanker', for whatever reason; be it injury, fitness, not liking the lifestyle or just plain being a wanker.

This was a very good motivational factor for me to dig in hard and stay. I was very fit and able to outrun most of my troop, which impressed the training team who would then pick on someone slower. I did not want to return home to my schoolmates in disgrace or disappoint my family.

The methods used to encourage greater accuracy in map reading were novel, to say the least. When, for example on Dartmoor, if you were more than ten degrees out on any bearing, Corporal Thomas from our Directing Staff (DS)[5] would stand the inaccurate map reader in front of the other members of the section, who would then 'jobby' him with sheep shit.

'Beasting' was another motivational exercise. If the troop didn't perform well enough, then it was common to hear, 'To that tree and

---

4. Nod: Slang for trainee or someone not long out of training.
5. Directing Staff (DS) refers to the Royal Marine instructors.

back. GO!' And we would all sprint off. This could be adjusted to match our ever-growing level of fitness. Often, when on Dartmoor, the cry of, 'to the top of that tor and back. GO!'[6] The distance and terrain would directly match the scale of the misdemeanour.

The first six back would stay, and the rest would go again. It was a gamble to go for it the first time, but invariably on the second run, I would pull out all the stops and ensure that I got back in the second six, then sit back and watch the rest huff and puff up the hill and back again.

The training was all the things they mention in the brochure that make the Royal Marines an elite force. Everyone finds it incredibly difficult in some areas, but if you have the right mental attitude you can get through it.

---

6. Tor: Small rocky mountain.

TRIP FLARE CHAOS

As training progressed, the exercises got longer and longer; more nights were spent out in the field, with longer distances to yomp and shorter times to have something to eat and get your kit in order before the next yomp. There were programmed activities on a seemingly endless schedule of training. Time to crash out got shorter and shorter, as the training team had a vast number of techniques to piss you all around. And if it all went wrong, the tors to run up got higher and higher.

This sleep deprivation was a necessary and accepted part of training. Over time, you gained the ability to crash out in the most uncomfortable of places for the shortest imaginable time periods.

Any lift in transport = sleep.

Any tea break longer than five minutes = sleep.

The worst time to practice this art of sleeping on a clothesline was during a critical part of any exercise. Invariably, someone would test this 'worst time' theory at the most inappropriate moment possible.

One night, after a few days on Dartmoor and a 9-mile approach march, we lay up in an ambush point. All had gone well with the recce[7] patrols, and everyone had acquired good positions to surprise the 'enemy'. If they were foolish enough to pass the ravine in front of us, then we were ready to wipe them out

Trip flares had been laid to illuminate the enemy in the 'killing zone' to our best advantage. Cut-offs were in place and we lay there in total silence for an unknown number of hours awaiting any passing enemy patrols.

---

7. Recce: Short for Reconnaissance.

The training team spent this time moving around the position silently, giving hints and tips to the section leaders and repositioning the machine guns to the best advantage.

Corporal Devaney crept along the line, checking that each nod was in contact with his neighbour and that all were alert. I became aware that he was lingering off to the right about three people down the line, in the position where Adi Towns was located. Unknown to us, Junior Marine Adi Towns had dropped off to sleep, but Corporal Devaney was well aware he had crashed out. I could hear him curse in hushed Scottish tones that his desire to carry out loud personal violence on Adi was being frustrated by the appearance of the enemy out of the darkness, moving stealthily into the killing zone from the expected approach direction.

Corporal Devaney took the decision not to bugger up the exercise for all by losing it with one sleeping individual. He knew that ripping his arms off and beating him around the head with the soggy ends would have made too much noise and alerted the enemy patrol. Instead, he gently bent down and removed the rifle from the arms of the sleeping Towns, who was too busy pushing the zzzzzz's out to notice and stood back behind him to observe.

He also took out a thunder flash (a loud military firework 'banger'). As the enemy got deeper into the killing zone, we waited for the section commander to tap the machine gun team on the shoulder, the signal to let loose with all blank firing weapons and trip all the flares.

Corporal Devaney, however, had other ideas. Standing with Towns's rifle in his hands, he struck a thunder flash and placed it tactically about 2ft from Towns's right ear.

BANG!

Off went the thunder flash, bringing Towns abruptly out of the land of nod. 'Open fire!' shouted Devaney at the top of his voice, as GPMG (General Purpose Machine Gun) and all other weapons opened up in a terrific crackle of small-arms fire. Further thunder flashes exploded as trip flares lit up the unfortunate enemy, who, in reality, would have been permanently horizontal in seconds.

Off to my right, I became aware of a figure lit up by the trip flares, running around in a crouched position, fingers sweeping the ground in ever-widening circles searching for his rifle. His eyes were wide open and gleaming in the trip flare lights. The expression, 'Flapping like a bastard' seemed to be the correct term to summarize the situation.

Corporal Devaney stood back in the shadows, proud of his successfully laid ambush but prouder still of Junior Marine Towns's rifle in his hands as he observed the gibbering recruit running up and down the ambush line.

As the noise of the ambush died down and the troop swiftly prepared for any follow-up action, we could hear a triumphant Scottish voice shouting, 'Towns, where the fuck is your rifle?' At the same time, the owner of the voice was calculating the quickest route to the highest Tor on Dartmoor.

THE MOUNTED ROYAL MARINE

Throughout the 360-year history of the Corps, the Royal Marines have deployed from ship, rowboat, truck, helicopter, parachute and submarine, and an armoured group drove tanks up the D-Day beaches. Royal Marines used pedal cycles to get to Pegasus Bridge from the same D-Day beach, and have certainly yomped over every known terrain on the planet.

However, there is one type of transport that delivers a combatant into battle that seems to have been eluded by the Royal Marines, and this is the horse.

RM Artillery must have used horses to pull carriages, but in all the books I have read and the research that I have done, the Royal Marines don't appear to have been involved in any full-on cavalry charge. By this I don't mean they have never used horses in battle, but nothing like the heroic Charge of the Light Brigade cavalry charge into the Russian guns in the Crimean War.

This is understandable, as horses and landing craft don't mix well, but that didn't put off one officer from bringing a touch of equine skill into the training arena of Commando Training Centre RM.

It was unbeknown to us nods, standing to attention awaiting inspection on the CTCRM parade ground during the cold winter of 1978/79, that the inspection Parade Adjutant, Lieutenant Gardiner, had quite an equestrian background. He was not riding a horse on the parade ground *just* to keep his shiny boots clean.

He had served in the Royal Marines since 1968 and had won a Distinguished Service Medal for Gallantry in Oman during the Dhofar War. He spoke with a confident, clear, crisp Scottish accent that could make a nod swell with pride if he were to cast his gaze over their uniform and simply say, 'Good turnout', before moving on to the next rank.

Somehow, from his mounted vantage point, he could also spot the smallest speck of Brasso negligently left in the corner of a set of brasses by some careless nod, and comment from his lofty position, 'honking brasses, extra parade'. That would cause the negligent nod to reconsider his whole future in the Royal Marines.

Having had the taste of desert warfare, I think he believed that he was cut out for that type of warfare, but was born just too late to have been a Lawrence of Arabia-type character who would have been the thorn in the side of German and Turkish forces in the Middle East during the First World War on mounted desert raiding parties. However, that impossible dream was not going to put him off riding a horse around a Royal Marine parade ground in 1978. One day, if he kept his cavalry skills up, he may yet lead Royal Marines into battle on horseback.

He had a whole set of lines to deliver to get his point across that some were underperforming and should consider taking their opt-out from his Corps and all the proud traditions it stood for.

His horse was named Benjamin, and he was a very well-trained parade ground mount; most likely a reject from the Household Cavalry, due to being slightly the wrong shade of chestnut. Otherwise, he looked like a superb charger.

'Your boots could not be more heaving if Benjamin had just shit on them,' he would quietly inform a quivering nod, whose disillusioned drill corporal would have a pen and a very long list of defaulters from the already-inspected ranks and still have the rear rank to go. The drill corporal was no doubt considering that he should have bought a bigger notepad, and maybe he should transfer to heavy weapons instead.

On Pass Out Parades,[8] Lieutenant Gardiner used to lead the King's Squad out in front of the Royal Marines band, saluting visiting dignitaries with his sword drawn as the King's Squad marched past, 'Eyes Right'. He did this impressive performance for my Pass Out Parade in June 1979 with 240A Troop as we headed off to our new duties.

I next saw him leading from the front again as Company Commander of the outstanding X-Ray Company of 45 Commando as they yomped

---

8. Pass Out is when someone graduates from training.

through our position at Teal Inlet in the Falklands. Heads up, massive bergens on their backs, they were festooned with weapons as they made their historic 75-mile yomp towards their fate on the Two Sisters mountain feature another 20 miles in the distance. He wasn't riding his horse at the time, but the raiding parties his company carried out and the outcome of the final mountain battle were equal to any legendary desert action carried out on horseback or camel against armoured trains.

His successful career continued to the rank of brigadier, but on his way up he was also the CO of 40 Commando on his fourth tour of Northern Ireland, and was Equerry to The Duke of Edinburgh for a time too. His unputdownable book, *The Yompers*, describes his time in the Falklands with X-Ray Company. Just the sort of leader a Commando unit needs in battle.

TESTING COMMANDOS

We had 15 miles left to go on the 30-Miler commando test across Dartmoor. Running with full fighting order and rifle, we had eight hours to complete this test, navigating across tussock grass and track as a section. The section had to move as one and complete the arduous task in time to pass the last of the commando tests and achieve the honour of wearing the coveted Green Beret. We were coming off the worst part of Dartmoor and onto more passable tracks. We had a long way to go, but I felt good and knew that I would pass this test so long as I did not seriously break a leg. A minor break and I think my determination and mates would get me through that stage of training. I was at the fittest of my life.

I had only just recovered from a leg infection that I had picked up on the previous exercise, which had put me in sickbay for three days. The medics looked doubtful when Corporal Devaney visited me and enquired whether I was loafing off or was really injured. He had stood me out front of the troop when we got back to CTC after the long yomp back from the previous exercise and had given me a hard time for, in his eyes, trying to pull the wool over the training team's eyes. He had doubts about whether I could hack it. I had been in real pain for the last couple of days, and although I had completed the forced march home, I had not performed to my normal standards at the front of the troop, setting the pace with the leaders.

Corporal Devaney sensed that maybe here was a bloke who was going to give up just at the end of training, as he had seen before, so made an unfair example of me.

The medics explained that it was a potentially serious infection, that I may not be fit for any further running for several weeks and would remain 'turned in' for several days. The doctor then turned to Corporal Devaney and enquired, 'You haven't made him run anywhere over the last few days, have you? As that would have exacerbated any injury.'

Corporal Devaney put on his best, slightly higher pitched voice and stated, 'No Sir, we wouldn't have done that.'

As he looked at me, I think he realized he had been wrong over the past several days about my performance. I said nothing and Corporal Devaney left sheepishly. But I considered that he would not report back favourably to the training team on my behalf.

I had therefore missed the Tarzan Assault Course pass-out commando test as I had been in sickbay, but made a good recovery with lots of painful antibiotic injections every four hours and made it to the start line of the 30-Miler several days later with my 240A Troop. Even if I passed the 30-Miler now, I still had the Tarzan Assault Course to complete in King's Squad in a week's time if I were to pass out with 240A Troop. If I failed the 30-Miler or the Tarzan Assault Course, I would certainly be 'back trooped' and not pass out with 240A Troop and my fourteen remaining originals (remember that I started with sixty new recruits!).

On the last few miles of the 30-Miler, one of the lads, Taff, collapsed. Taff was our section diamond and a very mature 17-year-old. He was excellent at all aspects of Royal Marines training and was super fit. But as we neared the end of the 30-Miler, he appeared to almost lose consciousness and his legs went from beneath him. Corporal Thomas, who was accompanying us, was obviously very concerned, calling up the medic's Land Rover. Fortunately, we were by now on a track wide enough to take a four-wheeled vehicle and were not far from the finish, so one was with us in about five minutes. Corporal Thomas monitored Taff as we removed his rifle and equipment. It wasn't unusual to have someone take a fall and then recover once they had been given some water and five minutes of rest. We hoped this would be the case with Taff. We were well ahead of time, so even made noises about carrying him the last couple of miles. Once the ambulance Land Rover had arrived, Corporal Thomas got in with Taff and the medics, and they made their way off to the hospital at speed. Corporal Thomas told us to keep going 'that way', as the finish line was only just over the next bridge. With that, the ambulance doors shut and off they went. We quickly formed up again and legged it towards the finish line on the tarmac road leading towards the stone bridge and the finish.

On we yomped, actually increasing speed on the last section, and completed the 30-Miler in six hours and forty-five minutes. Wow! Relieved to have finished, we sat around with large mugs of tea against a wall, boots off and with hot pies in hand. The silver lining had been taken off, though, as we were very concerned about Taff. I also had a Tarzan Assault Course yet to pass in the next few days, so whilst my mates started to consider what it was actually going to be like in a real commando unit, I was focusing on the high ropes and netting of the assault course.

When we got back to camp, the troop learnt that Taff had actually collapsed with kidney failure and was now in intensive care at the hospital. We were in shock, as were the training team. Although they tried to hide it from us, we could tell that they were quieter and more concerned about their popular junior marine who was so close to being their fellow Green Beret colleague but was now in hospital fighting for his life.

Taff did eventually make a full recovery and did attend the Pass Out Parade, but in a wheelchair with his family on the side of the parade grounds. I think it was a very rare thing, but Taff had performed so well throughout training that he was going to get the King's Badge for best all-around recruit from the training team. Everyone considered that he had pushed himself to his limits and couldn't have put in more effort than almost dying, so he was allowed to pass out having completed 28 miles of the 30-Miler.

Unfortunately for Taff, he did not get the King's Badge, but he did join 42 Commando several weeks later, a fully trained Royal Marines Commando.

So it was with this set of events that I found myself at the start of the Tarzan Assault Course three days later. I had been planted in with the troop just behind us, along with some other back-troopers that were from the troop who had already passed out. This was their third go, and if they did not pass this time, they were most likely going to be back-trooped several months or end up kicked out.

The troops who were on their first go were all hyped and their training team ensured that they did not mix with the quieter, subdued bunch over to one side, that I had been put in. They seemed to stand around staring failure in the face. I was OK with this test as I had completed a passable time during a practice a few weeks ago, and so long as I didn't fall off anything, I felt I could pass on this day, my first actual attempt at the Tarzan Assault pass-out.

I was checking my equipment and webbing, picking up a rope strop to use on the death slide, and was just about to climb the steps to the first obstacle when Corporal Devaney turned up and walked straight up to me.

'All right Lewis, I am gonna run round with you. Make sure you get around,' he said with a slightly menacing tone, which I was unable to decipher as a good or a bad thing.

I launched myself off the platform and started the descent down the death slide. Three other re-runs had all gone before me, and the troop who were on their first pass-out run were queueing up behind me.

I swung once, made a perfect dismount and charged towards the next high obstacle. I overtook one of the re-runs in front of me on the changeover point on the high obstacles and attacked the next net. I was met by Devaney as I started the 400-metre run to the start of the assault course. Devaney dropped in beside me, and it was only then when he said, 'Come on Lew, let's catch up with that wanker in front', that I realized he was on my side and wanted me to pass today.

I was too focused to consider that he was, in a strange way, saying he was sorry for slagging me off in front of the troop after the final exercise.

My only focus was to pass this last Commando test, and I could do it in the next few minutes if I kept the pace up. I overtook the second re-run just before the 6ft wall and ran straight at the wall, timing my footwork so that one pace before I slammed into the wall full-force, I would place the next step one-third of the way up the vertical surface and gain the top in one movement, with my elbows on the parapet.

Out of the corner of my eye, to the right on the other side of the wall, I noticed the Commandant and some other senior officers observing the Tarzan pass-out with a senior PTI (Physical Training Instructor).

As I placed my foot on the wall about a third of the way up, I felt Corporal Devaney put his hand on the pouches on my belt and give me one huge heave up into the air.

I went over the wall like Sergeant Angel goes over the fences in the film *Hot Fuzz*. I placed one hand on the parapet as I went over and landed as best as I could, and kept running. The Commandant and senior officers looked amazed that this recruit had just vaulted the 6ft wall in one go in front of them. The senior PTI spotted Corporal Devaney and looked him in the eye as Devaney saluted the Commandant and visiting brigadier before joining me at my shoulder again as we headed towards the monkey bars, where the next and last target re-run was about to be overtaken. Up the 30ft wall after that and I was finished.

I stood up, hands on my hips, getting my breath back at the top of the wall, where another PTI stood with a stopwatch.

'Do you think you passed?' he asked.

'Yes, I think so. But what's my time, corporal?' I replied.

'Yeah, you did well. 10.45. Now get down to the ground and fall in.'

Yes! I had passed with a couple of minutes to spare. I climbed down the ladder steps and was met by Corporal Devaney at the bottom.

When I told him what time I got and that I had passed, he just said, 'Well done Lewis. Now get yourself back to the grots, shower and join the rest of them on the parade ground for King's Squad.'

He turned and never said a word to me for the rest of training about the hard time he gave me in front of the troop, my injury or the launch over the 6ft wall. It was done, as far as he was concerned.

KING'S SQUAD TO CLERK'S COURSE

Gosh, we looked smart and were bursting with pride as we marched around camp on King's Squad week. Maybe the recruits in training were just too busy to take much notice, but I do remember looking admiringly at previous King's Squads during the last nine months and found it hard to imagine myself in that position. We had a simple white lanyard depicting outwardly that we were the King's Squad, but our turnout and bearing signalled this fact far more decisively than the lanyard and chinstrap worn down. We seemed to part recruits as we marched up steps and down the main drag.

We were getting notified of our postings that week, and most had just been told from a list that they were going to 42 Commando or 45 Commando. I, along with two other marines, was told to come to the office separately and speak to the troop commander. What was this about? A special mission? Maybe bad news, and we were not going to pass out for some unexplained reason? Being called into the office was only usually bad news, and I had managed to avoid it for all of the last nine months.

Lieutenant Hudson addressed me curtly, 'Junior Marine Lewis and soon-to-be Marine Lewis, I have called you into the Office to inform you that you have been nominated for a clerk's, or C3 course, after training. You will still go to 45 Commando first but when the course is available, you will attend Lympstone again and become a C3.'

I was devastated. I had done all that was asked and more of me. I wanted the brochure lifestyle of a Royal Marine and to do all the action-packed things we had got a taste of in training, not sit in an office and work through paperwork and type orders.

Lieutenant Hudson, the troop commander, could see that I was not happy. It was only the second time I had felt like crying in training. The first time was on an arduous five-day exercise at the beginning of training, when we were told we had to do the night Navex again because we had done so badly on the first attempt. Cold, wet and hungry, we were going through the mill and the selection process. But this was different; I was getting detailed off as a clerk and was powerless to do anything about it.

I politely told the troop commander that I did not want to do this by any stretch of the imagination, but he informed me that three marines from each troop that passed had to supply one signaller and two clerks as they were desperately short of them, and no one in the commando units was putting in for the courses, unsurprisingly. I think the powers that be knew that the point of least resistance was a marine straight out of training.

'Look, Lewis, we don't like doing this either, but you and the other two detailed off were the only ones in the troop with O Levels and who can string a decent sentence together in writing,' Hudson replied. 'So that is final. You have got 45 Commando, which you put in for, and will go to a fighting company first for a few months. That's as good as it gets.'

What could I do? Fail it? Leave the Corps? I was still two months shy of turning 17, so I could just ask my Mum to opt me out. I was not keen on that option and did not even think of threatening it. I was too scared they might just say, 'OK, go then.'

On reflection, I think it was a bit to do with my exam results but was more actually to do with the needs of the Corps at that time. I heard some later got detailed off for chefs' courses. I also think Lieutenant Hudson was looking after me as I was still a very fresh-faced 16-year-old, and to not put me in a troop with the monsters he had only just come back from trying to control in 45 Commando was actually the kindest thing to do with a boy soldier. Let the sergeant major or chief clerk keep an eye on me until my eighteen months of clerk's service were up. I had a whole career ahead of me, and a few months learning how the Corps worked was all good stuff as far as he was concerned.

The Duke of Edinburgh was the senior officer to inspect and pass us out. What a day and what an honour! It all went well. Families were invited along, the training team chatting up our older sisters, and there were big eats all around. The Royal Marines band played faultlessly, and we were led off the parade ground to our future duties by Benjamin and the mounted officer, who was considering whether his Arab Keffiyah headdress would add to the flair of his highly polished boots and drawn sword at the next King's Squad parade.

NOD TO SPROG

My first draft was to 45 Commando, which I had put in for when I passed out as it was the unit my Dad was in. When he was in 45 Commando, they were on draft to Singapore, Cyprus and The Middle East; now they were based on an old RAF airfield with Second World War Nissan huts in the less-exotic, rundown Scottish fishing town of Arbroath.

After a 600-mile rail journey, I arrived on a typical Scottish summer's day of grey skies and light drizzle, with a difference of 10°C in temperature between the North and South of Britain.

'Condor?' the taxi driver asked as I lugged my suitcase and pusser's[9] kitbag into the boot of his Ford Cortina, making the suspension dip by several inches.

'Yeah, 45 Commando barracks,' I confirmed in a non-too-confident voice, not wishing to give the game away that I was fresh 'out of the box' and unaware that Condor Barracks was in fact 45 Commando's base.

'You new then?' was the driver's next line as we made our way out of the built-up area of Arbroath. Within only about three minutes of driving away from the station, we were heading along a dead straight road at breakneck speed which led to the old Second World War airfield that now accommodated 45 Commando.

'*How could he tell I was new?*' I thought to myself. I had grown to 6ft during training and could yomp all over Dartmoor without catching my breath. My hair had grown slightly longer whilst on leave, so I couldn't

---

9. Pusser: Navy slang for anything belonging to the Royal Navy (therefore including all Royal Marine kit and systems).

possibly be mistaken for a nod. The driver seemed to talk in statements rather than using conversation starters, making the sound of the last word curt and raising his voice slightly, leaving his passengers to just confirm or deny the fact. Maybe it was years of running drunken marines back to Condor Barracks who were too pissed to do anything other than grunt.

'You'll be joining the rear party then?' was his next statement. I didn't know how to answer this; we had been told in various briefings not to pass on information to just anyone we met about troop movements. I knew that the unit was on exercise in Denmark, but could I risk confirming this major NATO exercise and the posting of Marine PO38135K Lewis to the rear party of Condor Barracks to this driver, who seemed to know everything anyway or else was a very cunning Russian spy?

I grunted a non-confirmatory reply in the hope that this wasn't a test and felt relieved to arrive at the main gate of Condor Barracks, both from the point of view of no longer having to try to make progress with any conversation or guard against giving away any NATO secrets.

'You'll be paying me two pounds fifty,' was the driver's closing statement as he left me to heave my kit bag and suitcase out of the boot.

Seeing the familiar Green Beret guarding the main gate, I said a cheery, 'Hello.'

'You new then?' the main gate sentry stated in the same accented voice as the driver.

I walked into Yankee Company's accommodation block and was met by a bunch of old sweats sitting around a TV. Upon enquiring where room six was, one of the 26-year-old 6ft-2 marines looked me up and down and said, 'Give us a chew skin' (a naval term for a certain phallic practice).

I found room six on my own whilst the group around the TV chuckled to themselves and felt good, having just intimidated yet another new sprog.

Things settled down, with a pecking order being quickly established. If you had done less than five years you were a sprog and shouldn't try to engage in conversation anyone who had been in longer than you. There was no point in idle conversation with any of the older hands, as they'd just give you the flick. This tended to cause the newer lads to hang around with each other, otherwise you would probably never talk to anyone. One evening, after some three months at Condor, I was settling down to a book and maybe a trip down to the NAAFI with some 'oppos'[10] later, when Jock Reynolds arrived at my bed space. Jock had been in the Corps for years and was a well-respected old sweat of the company.

'You coming ashore, Lewie?' he asked in a broad Glaswegian accent.

'No,' I replied. 'I'm staying in tonight, but I might go down to the NAAFI later.'

I was rather surprised that Jock would request my company on a run ashore, but I also made the error in assuming it was not a request. Jock raised an eyebrow, took hold of the padlock on my locker and pulled it off the doors, then threw my shoes and a T-shirt at me and demanded, 'You're coming ashore', this time with less patience in his voice.

'OK,' I said meekly, putting my shoes on and following him out of the room. Several hours later, after far too much beer and generally being told, 'You know what – you're my best mate, you are' by a number of the assembled old sweats of the company, I realized that I had finally become accepted and a whole new life was thus opening up for me.

This new life started with someone setting the 'ferret' onto me – a nice local girl who could sink a pint faster than Jock Reynolds. She also seemed to like 'the jolly old thing', but obviously wasn't into long-term relationships.

_____

10. Oppo: One's opposite number, best friend, companion, wingman, team-mate, etc.

THIS WAS WHAT I JOINED FOR!

This is what it was all about! Fresh out of training and embarked with 45 Commando Royal Marines on one of Grey Funnel Line's oldest and most ferrous-streaked vessels, HMS *Bulwark*, a Commando Assault Ship.

Rumour had it that with all the chipping and painting, which was a permanent pastime of the 'matelots[11] on board, there were so many coats of paint that it was the only thing that held the ship together, and also made it float several feet lower than designed.

We were heading for Gibraltar and the Mediterranean; foreign travel, historic sites, new cultures, helicopter and amphibious assaults … this was what I had joined for!

As the ship steamed on, the older hands in the unit were telling stories about previous outrageous runs ashore that they had enjoyed in their younger days on 'Gib', which as normal led on to other older marines cutting in and describing runs ashore in Singapore and other far-flung places the Corps had taken them to in the 1960s and '70s. Us sprogs looked on and listened in; some were bored of hearing the same stories again and again, but were polite about it and kept quiet. Others actively got on with mess deck entertainment, such as card schools and 'uckers'. All, however, had doubts on the full validity of the stories. Surely if they had really got up to all those antics, they would either have been kicked out of the Corps or be dead.

Uckers is a traditional mess deck game based broadly on the children's game of Ludo, only more violent. Uckers boards have been known to

---

11. Matelot: Fifteenth-century French word for 'sailor' which made its way into British slang.

frisbee across the mess deck when tempers have flared, narrowly missing the participants of nearby card schools.

Other groups sat on lower bunks chatting, slowly drinking their beer issue of two cans per day, per man, as the ship ploughed on into the night, bunks and loose fittings rattling away.

Shore leave in Gibraltar would be a simple-enough exercise, you would have thought – the ship docks, ropes tie us to the shore, all go ashore and have fun.

But no, the Navy seemed to like having rules about every aspect of their sailors' lives, and also seemed to take great delight in imposing these rules on us Royal Marines (or Royals). I concluded that it was done just to bugger up an otherwise enjoyable experience. The Regulators (or Reggys, frustrated sailors who weren't all that clever at navigating or firing missiles, so they were selected for the Navy's Police Force) would stand on the gangplank, signing matelots and marines in and out. A favourite pastime of Reggys was to display their limited knowledge of naval law and inform anyone who would listen that they could, if they so wished, lock you up for the most minor of misdemeanours such as being drunk, attempting to cast-off French naval vessels moored nearby or getting caught by foreign police forces.

Before shore leave was granted, the traditional Rock Run was carried out to the top of the nearby mountain and back to the ship. The whole commando unit and most of the ship's company took part in the Rock Run (apart from the Reggys, who had more important duties to perform, similar to that of nightclub bouncers, standing around looking menacing and feeling very important). The Rock was a very steep and tiring run on the way up, and an uncomfortable 'slip slap' of size 12s on the way down if you let gravity take you away. Between bouts of heavy breathing, I managed to look at the views and plan a tour of some of the historic sites I thought I would like to visit, before no doubt having a few beers in the evening.

So ashore it was with half-a-dozen lads from the unit, some with a similar amount of service as me and others who had been in as long as four years! I remember muttering something about visiting the historic caves, the taking of Gibraltar from the Spanish by the Royal Marines in 1704 some 300 years earlier, and being met with words similar to, 'Get your head down you culture vulture! We're going out to get harry crappers.' I took this to mean, 'We are not interested in sightseeing, we are going to the nearest pub.'

This also seemed a good plan, especially since George (a funny, friendly and good-looking 20-year-old Geordie with four years' service, who seemed to know everyone and everything about the Corps) knew a well-to-do family who lived on the Rock and had received an invite to bring some friends along and use their swimming pool. This was even better than expected, mixing with the rich and famous on my first trip abroad. I placed my tourist leaflets back in my locker, put on my best beer-drinking trousers and followed on like a small boy in a *Famous Five* novel. After a few beers in a local bar and the purchasing of a fairly impressive 'carry out', we arrived at George's friend's villa. We were even more impressed to learn when we arrived that a party was planned.

The house was a large, whitewashed affair set in its own grounds. At the rear was a paved area leading onto a fairly large and deep swimming pool with a springboard, and a disco set right next to the pool. The DJ, with headphones attached by curly wire to the deck, was selecting records from cardboard boxes on the large speakers which were blasting out the latest 'New Wave' sounds and some local music. Around the pool were small groups of people, including girls in bikinis, sunning themselves while pretending not to have noticed the fit, sun-tanned, good-looking young men who had just arrived (I think they really thought we were just idiots with far too much beer in plastic carrier bags).

After George had made the introductions, we got down to some serious drinking and bronzing. Wow, I had arrived; this was also what I joined up for!

As the party progressed, some of the smoothies in our group invited some girls over, who surprisingly agreed, and even more surprisingly started giggling when Smudge and George started using some quite dreadful chat-up lines. I could have used those lines to the same effect myself if I was a bit older, was shaving every day and had the looks and confidence of four years in the Corps. I felt in a similar position to being on a mess deck listening to old sweats' stories about Singapore again, with very little to add to the conversation but with a desire to join in. Particularly with the dark-haired girl in the white bikini who was completely ignoring me as she was transfixed by George's smile and annoyingly attractive blue eyes. Still, at least here there were other potential options open to a young Royal Marine rather than just an uckers board and cards.

Nearby was a group of matelots who had also conned their way into the party. They didn't have the foresight to buy a carryout and were looking enviously at the good-looking girls who were with our group (or perhaps our beer). At least *they* thought I was making moves and 'trapping' one of the girls, even if I knew I didn't stand a chance.

Smudge then decided to re-enforce his position as local Romeo and stacks rating (someone who always easily finds a willing partner when it comes to sex) by performing on the springboard. The good-looking bastard could also dive and do somersaults, surfacing without a hair out of place and hauling himself out with one smooth action, shoulders rippling, with a hard, muscular six-pack underlined by his swim shorts, only to try another even more ambitious athletic antic from the springboard. The girls were very amused when George joined in and started performing shoulder carries with both of them springing headfirst off the springboard and effortlessly separating before entering the water with a streamlined splash. This was going to be a good run ashore.

As the music continued to blare out, a shout was heard from one of the matelots. At the time, he was standing about 10 metres behind the stereo deck in a pair of cut-down jeans. 'Oy, Royal, you think you're so smooth, watch this bastard,' he shouted. He then ran at the disco deck at full pelt, arms and legs pumping away. As he reached a point about 4ft from the seated DJ, he took off with a jump and did the most impressive swallow dive right over the DJ's head. I can still picture the scene as he cleared the DJ, his face changing in mid-air from that of a determined athlete challenging the world record long jump title to that of a person reaching the top of a waterfall in a canoe and getting their first glimpse of the thundering water hundreds of feet below.

He opened his legs to go either side of the headphones worn by the DJ, but unfortunately he didn't swallow dive quite far enough, and his feet caught the record deck and speakers, tipping the whole shooting match into the swimming pool.

The DJ had a similar expression on his face as the curly wire on his headphones straightened out, unplugged and sprung back into his face while the matelot, along with his entire record collection and the majority of his sound system, disappeared into the swimming pool.

There was the most almighty bang, followed by complete silence as parts of the sound system smoked in the pool before slowly sinking. Everyone looked on as the unfortunate matelot did a mushroom float to the surface with arms and legs spread out, not moving. Fortunately, no one else was in the pool at the time.

Smudge used a pole and hauled him out, with all his mates looking on. Bugger! He was dead!

I was sure the Reggys would find some naval law we had broken, and we would all be in the shit. We made some strenuous but unsuccessful efforts to resuscitate, until hope had run out. An ambulance arrived and someone mentioned that the local police had been called. George then made the command decision that it was about time we left. Picking up the remaining beer that nobody else seemed to be interested in, we exited side left and headed back to town.

As we steamed away from Gibraltar and into the Mediterranean, the Captain announced the sad news that one of the ship's company had suffered an unfortunate accident whilst ashore and warned us of the dangers of mixing alcohol and swimming. That evening, George spun the story to the rest of the mess deck. The old sweats played uckers together on the prime seating areas of the mess deck, drinking beer from cans, semi-listening and politely smiling, no doubt silently questioning the validity of the story, thinking it couldn't have been as good as a run ashore they once had in Singapore.

OVER PAID, OVER HERE AND OVER THEIR HEADS

The chance to work with the Yanks was always relished. Generous, warm-hearted and friendly, they always arrived with loads of bright shiny kit to prof.[12]

My first experience of working with the United States Marine Corps (USMC) was on a joint exercise in Sardinia. One company of USMC was going to deploy with us on the exercise and we were going to do some cross-corps training. This meant that we got to use some of their equipment, including helicopter gunships, hovercrafts, tanks, quad bikes and their well-equipped stores department. In return, they got to try out our lumbering, ancient landing craft designed just after the Second World War and fire our 20-year-old rifles. If the Navy could arrange it, they also got a go in a clattering 25-year-old Wessex helicopter.

The USMC came on board our ship in the afternoon before the planned landings the following morning.

We welcomed them with a few cans of beer from our secret store built up from the daily issue of two cans per man. Little did we know that all American ships are dry. These guys had been on board for over seven months and had not had a drink in all that time. It was great fun as a 17-year-old to drink a 38-year-old USMC Master Sergeant under the table and not even dent your supply of beer. These guys were slurring their speech and wobbling their way to the heads within an hour. They all crashed out early and woke with huge hangovers the next morning,

---

12. Prof, proffing, proffed: To 'acquire a military resource' that isn't being used, or guarded, or isn't locked up. Basically, stealing with a smile!

not feeling a bit like boarding a flat-bottomed landing craft for the ride to the beach. We, on the other hand, arose early, ate the full 'ish' for breakfast and were our normal bright-eyed and bushy-tailed selves. This always pisses people off, and we milked it for all it was worth with our newfound friends, who could only grin and hope that the beach was not too far away. To their chagrin, the waves slammed against the flat-fronted landing craft as it tossed and rolled towards the beach and the moment when the cox shouted, 'Down ramp, out troops!'

Once ashore, it was agreed that we would also swap ration packs with our American friends. We duly handed over our twenty-four-hour ration packs and in return got 'C' rations, which initially seemed a bit disappointing until we realized that the green box, only slightly smaller than our daily ration pack, was in fact only lunch. Very nice too, we thought, as we tucked into the contents and realized why some US Marines were overweight, and that it wasn't down to the lack of exercise because they had been on a ship for seven months. Come teatime, my expectant American cousin arrived with his 'C' ration and handed it over, then stood there awkwardly, awaiting a gift in return. When it was explained that that was it until tomorrow, midday, he started doing one of those 'God darn man, you're kidding' speeches that Americans like to make when they can't think of a suitable counterargument.

This man had already 'traded' his Ka-Bar knife and USMC zippo lighter with me for a Royal Marines anodised shiny cap badge (price 18p from the stores department), and I thought it was about time he wised up. He had eaten most of the contents of my twenty-four-hour pack in one sitting, including the two packets of Rolos and two bars of chocolate, and was starting to worry about where the other 3,000 calories would come from for that day to keep him in the manner to which he had become accustomed. I could only convince him that I was not seeing him off when his oppos started the 'God Darn, you're kidding' form of remonstration with the remainder of my company.

He went off shaking his head, probably to pick up another 'C' ration from a huge pile nearby to where he was based. Now he understood why the British had bad teeth and were so skinny. I hoped he wasn't too upset, as I quite liked him and his slightly bemused, polite manner.

The following morning, as part of the cross-training, we headed for the beach, where the USMC build-up of stores was impressive: massive rubber fuel tanks full of petrol, with fuelling stations attached; beach masters using quad bikes, burger bars and cold Coca-Cola vending machines. We were, I suppose, put to shame on the logistics front. We did, however, have more fun with the stores than the nervously smiling beach master, who anxiously watched us race around on the quad bikes, using his fuel depot as a roundabout.

A 4-mile speed march inland was the next item on the agenda. The USMC started off first, on what should have been a piece-of-piss basic run. We started off after the USMC Company, four minutes behind them. It was like a red rag to a bull. Some of our older sergeants, and certainly the sergeant major, were soon huffing and puffing, but were determined to catch up and overtake the Yanks. As we closed with the three marching ranks a short distance ahead, we started to see equipment abandoned on the roadside. First it was helmets and webbing, then anti-tank rocket launchers and eventually men. Exhausted and blowing like cart horses, they were giving up en masse.

Soldiers who drop out of speed marches always have a self-justified look about themselves as they walk along with hands on hips, trying to get their breath back, as if it was obvious that they would have made it were it not for the poor-fitting equipment or the soles falling off their boots. Most go into total denial that they are unfit knackers who are a disgrace to themselves and their unit. A totally out-of-character experience was being had by many of the US Marines in the lead company as we overtook them.

God it hurt! But we kept up the cracking pace all the way to the end of the speed march, and were clapped in by the US Marine CO and his staff waiting at the firing range. It was then our turn to collapse in heaps, but we were ensured a full recovery while waiting for the first of the US Marine Corps Company to arrive in an undisciplined gaggle, a significant distance behind us.

There are many T-shirts printed and worn by 'gun nuts' with macho sayings and slogans such as 'Train Hard, Fight Easy' or 'No Pain, No Gain'. Most of those gun-toting, body armour-wearing militia types are so obese that the only advantage they have is that their bulk forms a steady shooting platform. Most would get out of breath climbing a set of stairs, as they proved recently on the steps of the Capitol in Washington DC. It takes more than a camouflage uniform to make a man, and it takes more than the Second Amendment to carry a gun. The fact is, if you are fitter than your enemy you have an instant and unmatchable advantage over him. It takes weeks, even months, to get fit, and by that time a war can be over.

Marines and paras (paratroopers) in the Falklands yomped up to 70 miles across tussock grass and tracks carrying a full load of kit and ammunition. They had little option when the main bulk of the transport helicopters went down with the SS *Atlantic Conveyor* when it was sunk on 25 May 1982. They had no choice but to put their training and fitness into practice and start yomping. Otherwise, they would face an ignominious defeat and remain where they were as food and ammunition ran out. They took the option to yomp. This yomp was followed by intensive recce and fighting patrols on the features surrounding Port Stanley. They then fought several mountain battles and won a historic victory.

The Argies (Argentinian military), in contrast, sent out a few foot patrols a short distance from their bases, many of which were compromised and taken out by ambush or artillery fire. They then stopped all further patrols. Upon surrendering their 11,000 troops to a land force of 5,000, they must have wondered what secret tactics we had used that had trounced them so thoroughly. Just about all the Argy boots I looked at when selecting my pair of size elevens from the spare boots on the hillside positions had good unworn tread. Ours were falling apart.

The seven months at sea must have taken a toll on the very likeable and professional Corps of US Marines we were training with. Maybe some vast military forces become so big and unwieldy that they can afford to have large parts of their formations become dreadfully unfit because the firepower and backup are so great that they can stand a few casualties.

After a few days ashore, the exercise finished with a BBQ. The Yanks supplied the food, we supplied the beer, and Sardinia provided the venue and weather. A lot of last-minute trading went on and card schools were set up. Warnings had gone around from the sergeant major that anyone who was down any kit would get charged and have to pay for its replacement, no matter how good a deal they had haggled with the gullible but generous USMC. Trading or receiving of any weapons or ammunition was strictly forbidden.

The evening's entertainment started with a huge bonfire and music playing from loudspeakers on the beach. As we all got more and more merry, the spinning of 'dits' (heroic stories) got more and more exaggerated on both sides. This included silly stories to make each other laugh and bond as fellow marines. Some comparison of our joint history was also made, with references to the Korean War, where both US and Royal Marines stood shoulder-to-shoulder against the invading Chinese hoards. As the evening progressed, the big friendly USMC Master Sergeant, who had drunk another two whole cans that night and was starting to slur his speech, got quite emotional. He was trying to come to terms with how the United States, with its short but heroic past, which had made such a significant difference in the Second World War 2 – when its super-efficient and well-equipped Army played such a decisive role in the liberation of Europe, rolling up German forces before them – was now reluctant to engage in any international operations and was still coming to terms with their most recent experience of the Vietnam War, and the effect this had on the US nation.

He quoted the recent Iranian Embassy hostage siege that had been ended by the SAS with outstanding success earlier that year as an example of how British forces could still pull something out of the hat when required. The Americans could only offer up the example of the disastrous desert helicopter crash that had occurred as American Special Forces tried to rescue hostages from the American Embassy in Iran, wiping out the whole rescue team. This was America's most recent small-scale combat experience, and the US Master Sergeant was at odds with the operational effectiveness of his own armed forces.

At this time, only realistic anti-war films, such as *Apocalypse Now*, had been released for cinema audiences. *Rambo* and other macho films with Arnold Schwarzenegger hadn't yet built up a false sense of confidence in American society, and maybe even in foreign policy, like only Hollywood can. This is especially so if the Americans win, which they always did in any Vietnam War film, apart from *Apocalypse Now*. These films must leave a whole generation of young Americans wondering why, after such an apparently resoundingly successful military campaign in Vietnam, their countrymen suddenly all got into a few Huey helicopters on the roof of the American Embassy in Saigon, as the North Vietnamese tanks came rolling down the street towards the embassy gates.

As a nation, in 1981, they were not yet dipping their toe into any more conflicts; unless of course they were forced to with Russia, where the whole world was fairly confident that it would be an apocalyptic draw.

We lined up in sticks the following morning in preparation to board the helicopters that were flying us back to HMS *Bulwark*, lying a few miles off the coast. The move went like clockwork. Helicopters queued up like taxies and landed three at a time. Sticks of nine men quickly boarded, then they accelerated off the ground, angled nose down, rotors biting into the air, as they swung around and headed off, out to sea. A few minutes later, they would disgorge their passengers onto the flight deck, to be met by the matelot flight deck crew who swiftly shepherded the passengers away from the manic, noisy swirl of rotor blades and below decks to the quiet hum of the clean, well-ordered life on board an HM ship.

Maybe it was an angst of mine, but I always took the helicopter training seriously, especially when we did the 'helicopter ditching in the sea drills'. The thought of ending up inside a noisy metal box as it crashed into a cold stormy sea at night filled me full of dread. Every time I flew over open sea, I always made sure that my hand was placed on the exit door or window so that if the worst should happen, I could orientate myself by moving towards my hand and hopefully escape. Others I flew with always seemed so blasé about it. I remember looking out of windows and ticking of the hazards like a checklist as they decreased while we neared our landing area.

Safe take off. Good.

No collision with the nearby mountains. Even better.

The engine sounds fine, which is just as well because we are over the sea now.

Any mass of birds would have already flown south because it was now June, but that would not stop some lone bird striking one of the engines.

The flight is only a few miles out to the ship, if we crash now, and are able to get out, rescue should be with us very soon.

Read again, for the tenth time, the instructions on the window for emergency removal of the window.

Check the lever that removes the window is in place.

Approaching the ship, hope the pilot doesn't stuff us into the side of the ship.

Good, the pilot seems competent.

Hope the crewman sees and warns the pilot who is then able to react in time to any hazard on the deck.

Safe so far.

Touch down! The helicopter came to a wobbling halt and then settled.

Move to the door and hope that the rotor blades stay up in the air instead of being caught by a freak gust that causes them to dip down and cut our heads off.

Now, just don't run off the side of the helipad deck and plummet head-first into the sea like a nod!

I was relieved as we landed and wondered why I went through this mental torture every time I flew with 'Jack Airways'.

We were met by the matelot guide, who lined us up safely, a short distance away from the helicopter and near to the ladder taking us below decks. He then quickly returned to the flight deck to guide another stick to safety from another troop carrier just landing.

I stood and watched the goings on along the flight deck with the interest of a spectator. Like a child who has just delivered his one line in a school nativity play, I could now sit on the benches and watch the rest of the act. I was pleased that I had not been auditioned for the part in the play that involved a single but loud crash on the symbols.

The next stick piled off the Wessex helicopter, and the guide gave a huge double take as one of the passengers got out of the door.

It was George.

Having had a successful night of trading, he looked like an extra out of *Apocalypse Now*: full USMC combat uniform, US helmet and an M16 rifle slung over his shoulder. He swaggered off the flight deck in his high-leg boots like John Wayne, with the matelot following up beside him shouting, over the noise of the helicopter, something about 'Are you sure you caught the right cab?'

The sergeant major looked on, like the 'all-seeing eye'. He focused on George and made the decision on who was going to be the first on the duty roster for the galley pot wash the following day.

COTTON ON SERGEANT MAJOR

When you had passed out from training, the silliness of the parade ground discipline disappeared overnight. We were trained, disciplined professionals who had little need for that sort of thing. The only people who still took it seriously were sergeant majors and senior officers, and even then, it was only once in a blue moon – major generals' visits, Corps memorable dates and the like. We would all put our 'Blues' (No 1 dress uniform) on, polish our boots and medals, and try to remember how to do drill. We were helped in this activity by our unit drill instructor. A thankless extra role that some took more seriously than others.

On one such major general's parade, the Company Sergeant Major (CSM) was walking down the ranks just to make sure that his company, which he took great pride in, were all looking the part: adjusting hats slightly, asking others in a low voice to look up a bit, shoulders back, that sort of thing. He then came to stand in front of Marine Griffin. After a quick inspection, all seemed in order.

The major general was just about to start inspecting the first rank when the CSM, sharp-eyed as ever, spotted a blue piece of cotton hanging from one of Marine Griffin's pockets. 'You've got a huge Irish pennant hanging from your pocket,' he chastised him quietly, so as not to disturb the major general's parade. The CSM then pulled on the piece of cotton, which expanded slowly to 6 inches, a foot, 2 feet!

The blue cotton reel in Marine Griffin's pocket continued to unreel and wrap around the CSM's glove. Eye-to-eye contact was made, with all sorts of revenge being plotted. Tittering went on around the company ranks as shoulders moved up and down to stifled chuckles.

The general moved slowly closer.

Left with few options, the whole reel was now unwound around his glove whilst Marine Griffin stood there with his best poker face, thinking of the unit kudos he would gain from this and the next six months of weekend duties the CSM would give him.

Just before the general started inspecting the rank which Marine Griffin was in, the cotton reel ran out and the CSM moved on, somewhat flustered, the cotton wrapped around his right hand behind his back.

What a relief. The commanding officer hadn't noticed, and although the RSM seemed aware of something and was suspicious, he showed no outward concern other than raising an 'all-seeing eye' in the direction of the flurry of movement as the CSM marched smartly off to the side of the company to take the salute.

The general, as ever, was oblivious as he inspected the remainder of the company.

'Thank you, sergeant major,' the major general said. 'Good turnout.'

'Thank you, Sir,' the sergeant major replied, smartly saluting the general, who saluted back. All eyes of the small party couldn't help focusing on the bright blue cotton wrapped around the saluting brown glove of the sergeant major's right hand. The general was polite enough not to mention it, but, judging by the steam coming out of the ears of the RSM, it seemed that the company was not the flavour of the month.

On such visits by generals, it was the form for the general to inspect and talk pleasantries with every few marines depending on how much time he had. No doubt he had a list of 'bone' questions that he used on such occasions, and also unwitty quips that his entourage dutifully laughed at by numbers as they followed on behind.

If he happened to inspect a marine who had once worked for him whilst he was on his way up in the ranks, he was genuinely delighted to be able to talk about old times and ask about how the marine was getting on. The entourage were also obliged to feel genuinely delighted, and displayed broad grins and nods for the benefit of this meeting of old chums. On one such occasion, the general was inspecting the front rank.

'What's your specialization?' he said, addressing a young marine.

'I am a chef, Sir,' was his reply.

'Chef! We don't have any chefs in the Corps, just cooks.' He turned to the CO, just to make sure that joke was well received. As if rehearsed, the CO's party all laughed by numbers. The inspection continued. Upon inspecting the second rank, the general again engaged an older marine in intelligent conversation.

'What's your specialization?'

'I am a cook, Sir,' came the curt reply.

'Oh, yes,' the general said, 'and how long have you been a cook?'

'About three minutes, Sir,' came the witty reply, as all in earshot burst out laughing. Except the RSM, who only smirked as he considered it a suitable task that befitted taking the piss out of a visiting major general.

DESK BOUND

The clerks course at Lympstone was not too bad. It was certainly *not* what I had joined the Corps for, but so many senior NCOs seemed to think it was actually quite a good number and did their best to persuade me that this was the case; such as that there would be no going out in the field B Echelon[13] on any exercise, which would mean better rations and the ability to arrange decent transport that would actually turn up.

Maybe they'd had enough of these discomforts themselves and were just projecting their true feelings about their role in the Corps. For some of them, a warm office with unlimited tea was much better than standing on some windswept range ordering lined-out troops to 'load' and then 'unload' thirty rounds later.

I fell on my feet when I returned to 45 Commando and ended up being a company clerk for a super Warrant Officer 2 (WO2) named Fred Riley. Everyone called him Sir to his face, apart from the Company Commander who, very respectfully, called him Mr Riley. He was a frustrated ex-PTI, and although he would rather be bouncing around a gym somewhere, he had a few injuries. And although he managed to keep fit, he knew his days of leaping over vaults and boxes were over. Furthermore, the pension of a WO2 gave him much brighter prospects when he left the Corps in a few years' time.

---

13. There are three main Echelons. F Echelon is the forward fighting force engaging the enemy. A Echelon is their immediate backup with rations, extra ammo, cooking equipment, etc. B Echelon is a further backup with longer-term supplies, stores, workshops, etc.

Fred would start the day with a run, and being an inclusive bloke, invited me along, which I took him up on as it would get me out of the office. We got on really well and I learnt a lot about how a commando unit actually runs.

The Company Commander also looked after the young marines detailed off as storemen, clerks or drivers, and arranged regular 'walks' in the mountains with sandwiches and flasks, just to get us all out once in a while. These were genuine hikes in the Scottish mountains, with no kit or weapons, and lunch breaks overlooking a loch or mountain pass. Transport would actually arrive on time, as Fred had ordered it and the drivers were mates with those taking part in the activities. He also made sure standards were kept up, with full Arctic training and the chance to join in with any adventurous activities that the fighting companies were getting involved with.

I was unaware when I took on this role that blokes in the company who were several years older than me would come to me to ask for advice on how to fill in forms for various courses they wanted to attend. A quick word in the dinner queue that a para course had just come out and would be on orders the following day, meant that a keen marine could get his 'chit' in first thing and stand more of a chance of getting the sought-after place.

Some lads who struggled with maths could be given help with claims forms in the office and walk out smiling, heading towards the pay office as I added some extra items they did not know they could claim.

On reflection, a large number of Marines from my era joined from a very disadvantaged background or were perhaps dyslexic, which led to poor report-writing skills. I found I could help them with a more fulsome answer when they put in for courses, rather than leaving a question blank or worse an unintended trite reply such as 'The Corps needs snipers and I am a good shot'.

So, as a fresh-faced 17-year-old, who looked like he should still be at school and certainly not in a commando unit, I unwittingly built up a network of contacts and friends who would stand up for me if someone took the piss.

'Hey, I warn you, don't take the piss out of Lew. He has Fred Riley's ear, and you will find yourself getting some shitty draught,' they joked in some local bar as I drank orange juice, being too young to be served.

Even the relaxed barmaid wasn't going to jeopardize her licence on such an obviously underage child.

I got to know the sergeants' mess and officers' mess corporals, who would visit the company office with a few cakes for Fred and me, with their compliments. Visiting company commanders would get a reasonable cup of coffee and a cake. It all worked well, and I would have known nothing of this world if I had been digging a trench somewhere on some mountainside. I was also informed that if I cheerfully did my 'return of service' of at least eighteen months, then I would get looked after and pretty much have my choice of next draught or course. 'I can hack this,' I thought, as I set about diligently typing up another set of company commanders' orders with all the spelling correct.

SPECIAL SKILLS FOR SPECIAL FORCES

really enjoyed my time in 45 Commando. I spent about two years there. I was ski, mountain and Arctic warfare trained. I got a taste of life in a fighting company, along with learning about the HQ element. I had been on a sunny exercise around the Med and on an assault ship, and been to several new countries. More importantly, I made some great lifelong mates, with whom I am still in touch today.

Yet this was certainly not the 45 Commando experience my Dad had undergone. He had been covering the post-Second World War withdrawal from empire campaigns in desert shorts and jungle outfits. My time was very much the Cold War era, with the main threat being a massive Russian tank surge across the plains of Germany rather than my Dad's experience of keeping the lid on parts of the Middle East that we should have not meddled with in the first place, and should not meddle with again.

Northern Ireland was the main event for any likely active service. While that did not cause us fear, nor was it looked upon as a particularly attractive way to spend six months of your life trying to keep two diametrically opposed communities apart and prevent them carrying out atrocities upon each other.

Although I wore the same Green Beret that Dad had, I was now in a different era and most of the people he knew would have left, so there was no need to hang onto a nostalgic dream. I might as well make the best of my lot and see some more of what the Corps had to offer. Whilst waiting for nuclear Armageddon, why not improve my skiing technique, go on interesting courses or visit parts of the world I had never been to before?

During my time at HQ, I had gotten friendly with some carpenters who worked on the base. Here were four marines who seemed to do some very creative work that kept them busy all day, but also received respect from others in the unit as tradesmen. They seemed to be on the cake delivery list too. As much as I liked the company commander and Fred, they were several unobtainable ranks above me, and I was always going to be the tea boy in their eyes. I quite liked the idea of getting a skill for now and for my future, and to be honest, harking back to what Dad had advised. As well as joining the police, Dad had also supported the idea of being a carpenter.

So I changed my mind and put in for the Carpenters level 3 specialist qualification course at RM Poole. True to form and the unwritten contract, I got my next draught of choice and found myself with three other marines at Poole several months later. We were briefed and trained for the next six months by Darby, the Colour Sergeant instructor, on how to put up jungle encampments, make large constructions as well as useful things such as how to hang a door and make furniture with top-quality joints. We also learned to make presentation pieces for those leaving the Corps or for visiting dignitaries.

After this course, and whilst awaiting my next draught to 42 Commando, I worked in the carpenter's shop at RM Poole with a very skilled bunch of fellow marines. They set very high standards of professionalism in their trade, and I just did my best to learn and keep up.

I was asked by my sergeant to put together a few stores boxes for the Special Boat Service (SBS), who were based at RM Poole, so that they could keep their easily damaged specialist equipment safe when they put it on aircraft or other transport for their deployment around various world hotspots. I turned out a pretty decent set of custom-made boxes, and all the equipment, such as sights and listening devices, was safely stowed away as planned. They also requested a box and safe storage for their TV, VCR and video collections (mostly porn movies, or so it seemed) so that they could watch these in far-flung places and relieve the boredom between secret missions.

The SBS sergeant who gave me the specifications was very pleased and asked his old buddy, who was my current sergeant, if I could be spared to join his team in some leisure diving they had planned off wrecks and rocks in Cornwall in a few weeks' time. I nodded a hopeful 'Yes please'. I had always wanted to try some diving. So off I went a few weeks later, in civilian clothing and with lots of PE kit and running shoes, to join in with some diving with the SBS team.

As part of the Corps, the SBS are certainly something special, but they do just come from the ranks of the Royal Marines, and I had many friends who joined the service over the years. These guys were very relaxed and down to earth over the course of the week, and were very welcoming to me and the RM driver who had also come along for the experience. We stayed at a large holiday cottage on the cliffs not far from Land's End. There was nice company, good food and the chance to go diving. I had not been informed, but guessed that there would be a lot of running that week too!

The driver and I used a normal dive kit, but some of the SBS were using this as qualification time on rebreather sets. We were briefed and trained on each dive and had a fantastic time in the clear waters, diving on wrecks and seeing large conger eels poking their heads out of rocks and the abundant seabed life.

After one morning dive, the wind got up, making diving conditions too rough just offshore, but they had a great fall-back plan. We got the surfboards out of the back of the 4-tonner and had a beach afternoon instead. One of the guys, a sergeant in the Australian SAS, was a keen surfer. He showed me the basics, then I spent the best part of the afternoon trying to learn to surf. I got on quite well and even stood up a few times, but decided that on some large breaking waves, the bodyboard technique was going to give me a better ride towards the beach. I didn't stop when all the lads decided to lie on the beach for the last few hours. I just kept fighting my way out to sea against the increasingly large waves and then surfed back in non-stop. I considered that the guys must have done this so much that it was no longer a novelty, not thinking for one minute that it was a lack of fitness on the part of this Special Forces team. But they were all older than me, so maybe even they needed a rest from time to time.

One of the lads had brought his dog, Leo, with him for the week. Leo was a golden Labrador, and even he was under the shade of a surfboard having a kip.

As I carried my surfboard up the beach for the last time at the end of the day, the Aussie sergeant called out, 'Hi mate, you looked like you were enjoying yourself, you must be knackered.'

I had been so focused on surfing that it wasn't until it was mentioned that I realized I was indeed knackered and was looking forward to something to eat and a sit down in one of the comfy chairs at the holiday cottage.

It was as we loaded all the gear and surfboards onto the 4-tonner that I noticed all the guys were getting into their running shoes and shorts and putting their spare kit and bags into the cab of the truck. Leo was having a stretch and starting to liven up as if going for walkies. I asked when the transport was turning up, but Leo's master informed me that there was no transport; when they had a half-day's diving, they always ran back on the coastal path.

Christ! By road, it had taken us about a half-hour to get to the beach, but that did wind around inland quite a bit. I looked up towards the sand dunes that led to the South-west Coastal Path, the tiny track disappearing into the distance behind a headland.

'Oh right, of course. How far is it?' I asked, trying to sound nonchalant.

'Don't know really, but it must be 11 or 12 miles when you take into account all the headlands and summits,' he replied as he clipped the lead onto Leo's collar. Even Leo was looking longingly for the transport.

Bugger! I knew this lot were super fit, as I had seen them running all over Poole and the surrounding area at a steady champion marathon runner pace. I knew I could run that far, but it would have been nice to have a relax on the beach before the attempt of such a feat. I also felt my insides rumbling as I had taken in some seawater from being tumbled onto the shore when getting wiped out a few times when surfing.

Off we went at a steady pace as the 4-tonner pulled away, with my friend driving, saying that he would get the kettle on and the beers in the fridge for when we got back. 'I would run back too, but someone's got to drive,' he added, and off he went in a cloud of diesel smoke.

I have since walked many sections of the coastal path, and some of it can be quite challenging. Each time I have walked a section, one of my thoughts – in addition to not wishing to twist an ankle or fall off a cliff – has been, 'I'm glad that I'm not running this.'

I managed to keep up with the SBS lads for about 5 miles, then started to slow down but kept them in sight as their relentless and effortless pace saw them move ahead around rocky headlands and beach valleys. The next 4 miles were very difficult, and I slowed to a jog until I got to the road, where I thought I should turn left, but I had no real idea as they were nowhere in sight. I began to walk, thinking that if I passed a shop or garage I could ask for a drink of water and directions. My stomach then started to play up as the saltwater that had sloshed around inside let me know that it was about to 'get out and walk' from every orifice it could possibly exit via. I jumped behind a bush, dropped my shorts and opened up the sluices at both ends. Wow! That felt better! But I still had a few miles to go back to base.

I then saw the Aussie sergeant over the other side of the hedge. 'You alright mate? Got lost?' he asked in his thick Aussie accent.

'Yeah, I think I went the wrong way,' I replied, moving as quickly as I possibly could away from the stench I had just left behind the hedge.

'OK mate, I came back to see where you were. I will run back with you.'

'Great, thanks,' I said meekly.

Off we went at a steady pace again. I don't think the SBS know what a jog is. I kept this up for about a mile before slowing down so dramatically that the sergeant realized not only would he get bored at that pace, but more importantly, there was a beer with his name on it in the fridge, and the others would be reaching for the bottle opener about now.

'I'll see you back there; just keep running until you see the sign for the village.'

'OK. See you back there. Thanks for coming back,' I replied between breaths. I promptly began walking again as soon as he had gone around the next corner. After one more less-dramatic emptying of the bowels, I walked down the hill towards the holiday cottage.

I reflected that this was the one and only time since I joined that I had ever dropped out of a run, which I had mixed feelings about. So did my insides. However, I could surf now – after a fashion – and there was a cold beer waiting for me in the fridge. I hoped! And, of course, the SBS porn collection to watch into the early hours!

PROFFING

The jargon-buster lists 'proffing' as 'stealing with a smile'. The basic concept is that if it's personal property – either personal issue or personally owned – then to take it from a person would be stealing in every sense of the word, and the offender should get his fingers broken. But if it's left in the open and belongs to the stores department, or better still the stores department of another unit, then to 'prof-it' would be fair game.

There is no specific definition, because to give proffing a specific definition would mean that orders and regulations could be put in place to stop the practice and defeat the whole objective, and also close down a complete chapter of humour for future servicemen.

Proffing can also be used when there are lots of them, particularly if they are new and shiny. Officers turn a blind eye to proffing, while NCOs actively encourage it. If everyone benefits from some delicious delicacy or the troops are more comfortable as a result of some marine's ingenuity, then it's good for morale, especially if while eating or wearing the item, the consumer is aware that a rival unit is less well-fed or comfortable.

So the standard reply to the question, 'Marine Higgins, where did you get that US Marines truck from?', would be, 'Proffed it, Sir.' Everybody would get on board and be saved hours of yomping.

The opposite of proffing is 'dipping', hence the phrase, 'some prof and some dip'.

When working with the US Marines, I think they tended to dip more than prof, but they had so much shiny new kit lying around I don't think they ever noticed.

WHERE'S THE *STROMNESS*?

Date: 21 May 1982. Location: the South Atlantic.

It had started in March 1982 as a small BBC news story about Argentine scrap metal dealers and military forces landing on South Georgia, and progressed to a full air, sea and land Argentinian military invasion of a piece of British sovereign soil, with eighty or so Royal Marines fighting a losing retreat on the Falkland Islands. We sailed days later in April 1982 with a task force of Royal Navy ships and civilian cruise and stores ships. Was this to be our moment in Corps history?

The bulk of 42 Commando had landed the first morning of the operation at San Carlos Water, on the Falkland Islands, from the SS *Canberra*, using landing craft.

I was part of the reserve unit and remained on board until towards mid-afternoon, when, after many air raids, it was decided to get us off the ship and the *Canberra* out of the firing line, due to it being white and a huge target (it was nicknamed the 'Great White Whale' for a reason). I'm sure it had nothing to do with the potential cost to the MOD for replacing a sunken flagship of the P&O cruise line, nor the money spent on refitting the cruise ship into a troop carrier before it sailed from Southampton.

A small number of the company and I were left on board, having had an exciting couple of days watching the Argentine Air Force bomb lots of our ships and generally spread themselves over nearby hills when shot down. In the early evening dusk, we sailed for the open sea and the relative protection of the Task Force 200 miles east of the Falklands, beyond the range of land-based Argie aircraft. We cross-decked that night onto RFA *Resource*, a Royal Fleet Auxiliary ammunition ship that was due to head back into San Carlos Water the next day, in order to offload ammo at Port San Carlos as part of the stores and military build-up.

Now, call me Mr Fussy, but I didn't think that an ammunition ship was a much better prospect than a white cruise liner, having seen and experienced the accuracy of the Argentine aircraft the previous day. This ship had entire holds – the size of small hangars – full of boxed ammunition, mortars, 105mm shells, Sea Cat missiles and millions of small- arms rounds, all piled as high as the holds would allow. The crew even hinted that they had some 'big nasties' (i.e., nuclear weapons) on board, and that if the ship was hit, we wouldn't have to worry about the sovereignty of the Falkland Islands anymore because they probably wouldn't be there. At least not at that latitude!

The RFA *Resource* had loads of GPMG mountings on and around the rails of the ship. 45 Commando, which had gone ashore in the first wave but had sailed down on the *Resource*, had no doubt assisted the ship's engineers to make it bristle with these mountings. I think that the ship's crew were not just happy with supplying ammunition to Royal Navy vessels; they wanted to miss out the middleman and deliver it first-hand and, if a tactical situation arose, go on the offensive and nuke Argentina!

So we sailed back into San Carlos Water on 25 May. The anchorage looked the same, with beautiful blue skies, perfect for flying – ships all lined up ready to receive that day's air raids. We were anchored in between an RFA tanker and the RFA *Stromness*, another ammunition ship, a respectful distance from other supply ships and further still from Royal Navy ships that could be seen cruising around with missile launchers and guns swivelling.

Why were they not coming very close to us? We pondered why this might be as we stood at our machine-gun mounting between two boxed-up Sea Cat missiles, which were ready in rows to be flown off to resupply a frigate.

There was one Navy ship that was close to us, HMS *Antelope*, which had been hit whilst acting as 'goalkeeper' in San Carlos Sound and still had an unexploded bomb on board. It was tied up on a huge orange buoy whilst UXB teams tried to save it. That night the ship blew up, killing a bomb disposal officer.

I think that the bomb on board was one unfamiliar to the UXB team, Argentina having purchased arms from all over the Western world:

Type 42 destroyers, an aircraft carrier and 1,000lb bombs from us, Skyhawks from the USA and Exocet missiles from France. The UXB officer was unlucky, as HM Government had gone to great lengths to sell as many arms as possible to the right-wing Argentinian dictatorship. He could have had the relatively easy task of defusing one of our own bombs, but I think some German and Italian bombs were also dropped.

Another irony was that when the conflict started, we had no intelligence at all on Argentina's weapons. Intelligence cells were using Jane's military books to update us for briefings! We knew they had and could use their Type 42s, because not only had we sold the destroyers to them, but we had also trained their navy how to use them. The training teams were in fact with us, dotted about in ships of the Task Force, and they could confirm this. The best intelligence available was probably MOD invoices made out to 'The Argentinian Junta' sitting in files at Whitehall for all the weapons we had recently sold them.

HMS *Antelope* spent the whole day gradually sinking with its back broken, the angle between bow and stern gradually becoming more acute until all that was left was a small part of the bow peaking above the sea, still tied to the orange buoy. Neil (still a good friend today, whom I first met when he, as a lance corporal, had been detailed to find me a locker and bed space at 45 Commando) and I watched between air raids as it slowly settled, soberly commenting that there was a multi-million-pound Royal Navy ship actually sinking in front of our eyes. This sort of thing was not supposed to happen. We concluded that the last time a Royal Navy ship had been sunk due to enemy action was during the Second World War. Bloody hell; nobody was messing about, this was real and serious!

I remembered my five-minute lesson on anti-aircraft fire using a GPMG from training. It consisted of holding the GPMG at a 45-degree angle, and when a plane approached, you just fired and hoped that the pilot would fly into your stream of bullets. I don't think Corporal Thomas had the Argentine Air Force in mind during that lesson.

Being on an ammo ship, one thing we were not short of was bullets. Someone had mentioned that what seemed to be deterring the low-flying jets was the screen of tracer rounds that were being put up across the whole of San Carlos Water. Any pilot flying into this visible fan of red tracer dots could be put off during a bomb run, or may even get shot down.

There were also pom-pom guns and missiles firing at the jets, all adding to the pyrotechnic effect. The pom-pom guns were old Second World War guns bolted onto supply ships' gun mountings whilst on the journey down. On the RFA *Resource*, we had fourteen GPMG mountings, each manned by two Royal Marines; one to feed the rounds and the other to aim and fire. Our gun position was on the bridge wing of the ship, along with five other guns. From this high vantage point, we had a good field of fire and an excellent view of the battle. Below us on the deck down was an open area between the bridge and crew accommodation, where could be seen about twenty marines with just their rifles and sub-machine guns. All were fed up with being bombed, and whilst below decks someone had decided that it would be more fun to have a go back as well. They looked like a grouse-shooting party, all scanning the surrounding sky for a likely 'bird' to fly over to have a pop at.

The arrangement was for the goalkeeper frigates and destroyers, stationed in Falklands Sound and out at sea, to use their radar and give an 'air raid warning red' to the Task Force. Our own Harrier combat air patrols also gave early warning and would hopefully engage the Argentine Skyhawks and Mirages before they got to the Task Force ships and landing areas. When an 'air raid warning red' was announced over the ship's tannoy, we would start to scan the skies, with machine guns ready. Neil and I took it in turns to be No 1 on the gun. Some air raids did not develop, or they attacked other parts of the Task Force, and when we were stood down from these it was with disappointment that we headed off to the galley for a wet (a drink) and some freshly baked cakes.

We had decided that it would be a good idea to make up our belts of 7.62mm rounds consisting of complete tracers instead of one in two; much time was spent clipping these belts together, and the spare rounds were put back in the ammo boxes for the crew to dispose of. We considered that we would have more of an effect if this wall of red tracer went up from all weapons, and most gun teams followed suit.

The tannoy then announced 'air raid warning red', heralding our first air raid where we could shoot back. The crackle of small-arms fire could be heard further down the Sound. Bangs could be heard as missiles left their ships and arced into the blue sky. Neil and I waited expectantly, itching to shoot at a plane. Neil opened fire at 45 degrees, as per training firing into a clear sky. The Argie jets were somewhere because we could hear other people opening up.

Whoosh!

A Skyhawk flew almost at sea level right behind us as we fired our machine gun in completely the wrong direction. I could see the pilot wrestling with the controls as he manoeuvred his fast jet between ships and missiles, trying to stay alive while also attempting to set up a bomb run on one of the nearby ships. His afterburners came on and he beetled off over a hillside, twisting and turning.

It had all happened so fast; what chance did we stand against such fast aircraft? I don't think anyone had hit him. Someone excitedly told us of another plane that had accompanied the first one, but had flown even lower between the ships and therefore out of our view. We hadn't seen this one, let alone hit it. Rumour had it that if the pilots put on their afterburner to accelerate out of the Sound and danger, they would probably not have the fuel to get back to Argentina and would have to swim the last few dozen miles – clearly not a favourable prospect in the cold South Atlantic.

The number of air raids that developed that day didn't seem to confirm the afterburner theory. On the day went, with raid after raid, and numerous visits to the galley in between to sample the treats that the chefs were turning out. The crew helped us out in any way possible with extra ammunition and the construction of more complex gun-mounting brackets. By teatime, we were a bit full and some complained of getting stitches as they ran to their gun positions on yet another 'air raid red'.

Bob Frost was on one of the guns next to us. We had just got to our positions yet again and were awaiting the incoming raid. I heard Bobby mutter something along the lines of, 'Bugger this I've got to go.' He handed the gun to Ginge and went off with a purposeful stride to the nearby bridge wing head's cubicle. He locked the door levers down one at a time, as was the ship's procedure in action stations, and we waited for the next air raid.

Two dark shapes appeared over a nearby hillside, heading straight towards our location. No planes had yet attacked from this direction. The two Skyhawks hopped over the hillside and streaked down, contouring with the land to get as low as possible, just above the water as they accelerated towards us. Everybody opened up! But instead of the recommended and useless 45-degree angle, I was firing horizontally towards the two aircraft. I could see my tracer rounds and those from all the other GPMGs arcing from all sides, homing in on the likely course of the Skyhawks, about a mile away and closing rapidly. There was no doubt our ship, the *Stromness* and the tanker were the targets. One aircraft broke left and flew towards the bow of our ship, but remained at sea level, while the other climbed slightly and flew directly over the bridge. Just before it reached us, I saw two bombs leave the underside of the jet, and as if in slow motion, fall towards the *Resource*. The Skyhawk flew on straight over my head, and I continued to track it, as did several other gunners. I could actually see my tracer rounds hitting the plane and ricocheting off, while other tracer rounds were going through the wings and coming out at a different exit angle. I remember seeing and instantly recognizing the 1,000lb British military bomb as it followed the plane over my head, the dark green shark-like shape casing and the yellow ring on the nose designating this as British military high explosive. I was about to be killed by a bomb sold to Argentina by my own country!

One always imagines that when a bomb goes off nearby, it will make the traditional 'boom' noise, but louder. But when you're near or next to a bomb, it makes an almighty 'CRACK' noise, which combines with a percussion effect that makes you feel like you've been blown up even if you are lucky enough to survive. This was the feeling my colleagues and I had as a waterspout exploded higher than the ship's bridge. I was expecting the whole ship to explode in an instant chain reaction from the point the bomb had hit, which would cook off all the ammo underneath the decks, and we would all be vaporized, together with any nearby ships.

However, the two bombs had bracketed the ship. One landed in the sea near the bow and the other in the sea between the *Stromness* and us.

It all went quiet. I stopped firing. I think I was temporarily deaf, but I could feel the adrenaline surging through me: I could have jumped 100 metres clear over the rail if we had been hit!

The tannoy burst into life, the captain excitedly giving the crew below decks a running commentary on the air raids. 'We have just been bracketed between us and the *Stromness*; we have not been hit but a bomb has blown up between us and the *Stromness*.'

At this point, the bridge wing's head door levers opened quickly, one at a time. It was the first movement that anybody had made.

The door burst open and Bobby emerged with his trousers down, his face completely white and in shock. Behind him, we could see the inside of the toilet compartment covered in a thin brown substance which was running down the bulkheads. Bobby had a similar coloured smear all the way up his back.

'Where the fuck's the *Stromness*?' he wailed, as he stepped over the door casing and into daylight.

The pressure from the exploding bomb had blown back through the pipe work of our ship, forcing the entire residue back up from the previous occupants, pebble-dashing the inside of the cubicle and Bobby's back. The adrenaline stored up inside us had found a new outlet. We rolled about in laughter at our unfortunate mate, who made it even funnier by standing there looking hopeless, unable to see the funny side. The captain and crew on the bridge looked out to see what all the commotion was about. They must have concluded that we marines were truly mad. If any of the nuclear weapons on board the *Resource* had been hit, the Falkland Islands would almost certainly have been moved further away from South America, yet there we were in fits of uncontrolled laughter, tears running down our cheeks, while other parts of the ship were still in shocked silence.

The Skyhawk flew on and spread itself over a nearby hillside, leaving a satisfying black skid mark in the peat. The *Resource* was one of the few merchant ships to make a bona fide claim to downing an aircraft and get it confirmed.

The *Resource* had gone on the offensive.

GEORGE

When I joined 45 Commando at 16 years of age, I was the subject of much winding up, which is sometimes called 'biting', as you have taken the bait. Most bites are funny, but some of them would these days no doubt be recognized as bullying. Some people just can't stop themselves, and can make a new lad's life a misery. I never felt like this, but sometimes I sat silently, glad that the way others were being treated was not happening to me.

I put this down to George and a small bunch of good friends. George, Paddy, George and others accepted me as one of the group at a very early stage and took me under their wing, thereby making me more accepted within the wider group. George was just a thoroughly decent bloke. At 21 he was seen by some as an old sweat; he knew all the routines and everyone seemed to like him, the sergeant major and company commander included.

One day, George had been sent to collect the company commander's bike from the repair shop. Bikes were the main form of transport, as 45 Commando was located on a large old airfield with huge distances between buildings. George decided that the best method of collecting a bike was to ride there on another bike. This was great from the point of view of getting there quickly, but not such a good idea for getting back. This would require some trick cycling. That was no problem for the multi-talented George, as he rode one bike whilst holding the handlebars of the other.

As he rode back along the main drag, he picked up quite a pace, gaining greater confidence and speed as he neared the company office. Just then, the company commander and sergeant major came striding around the corner. George immediately felt that being seen by such distinguished officers, whilst riding both bikes in that fashion, could meet with disapproval; particularly since it was the company commander's bike he was riding.

The best way to defuse the situation was to fall back on training, and salute smartly and wish them both a cheerful 'Good morning Sir'.

This he did, causing him to let go completely of the handlebars of the spare bike. The spare bike then collided with the bike he was on, and George diverted off the road in a melee of wheels, handlebars and bits of turf, straight down an old air raid shelter dugout. He landed in a tangle of broken bike bits and mud.

'Fucking hell, George! At least wait for the company commander to return your salute before you dismount,' the sergeant major quipped between the two of them laughing at the display of stunt-cycling George had just performed. Being young and immortal, George survived yet another scrape with only a few bruises.

The company commander and sergeant major almost raced each other back to the office to complete Company Daily Orders in record time. The first item was, 'Any ranks interested in joining 45 Commando's stunt cycling display team to contact Marine George Davidson (currently attached to the Sickbay) for details. The first two volunteers will be issued with the newly refurbished bikes currently in the cycle repair shop.'

Eighteen months later, an air raid was coming in across San Carlos Bay. The ships in the Sound and bay had been the main targets so far. Many had been struck with bombs that had not gone off. HMS *Ardent* could be seen sinking in the distance, still moored to a large orange buoy with just the bow section above the water. Some of the stores ships still had unexploded bombs on board, where they had been dropped too low and had not armed. This arming was required to distance the fast jet from the explosion; drop them too low, and your bombs don't arm and therefore don't catch the jet in the explosion. Alternatively, a delayed fuse may have been fitted, designed to go off during the clear-up operation or when the bomb disposal teams were aboard. I found out later that this factor was heavily reported by the tabloid newspapers back home. I remember when I looked at old copies whilst on the journey home, they triumphantly stated, 'Argie's Drop Duds' or had similar headlines. They even included drawings of parachute retardant bombs that would do the trick. Thanks for pointing that out, we reflected.

All Royal Marines around the site of the Brigade Maintenance Area (BMA) were busy during these raids, taking pot-shots at passing aircraft. The build-up of stores at the BMA could not fail to be noticed by the Argies, with piles of ammo and commando medical squadron tents. Maybe they also read the *Sun*, as the day after the headline noted above, they came at us again.

This time they headed straight for the BMA. Marines working on unloading stores took cover in the nearest slit trenches. Laughing with nervous excitement as the four Argentine Mirages flew closer, it was proved that twelve marines into a two-man slit trench will go! The usual barrage of anti-aircraft fire rose from the BMA, everyone with rifles or GPMGs to hand joining in.

The aircraft flew over the BMA position, and again the slow-motion drop of bombs occurred. This time, parachutes retarded their flight opening for a split-second before impacting with a now familiar 'CRACK' and accompanying percussion that feels like you've been blown up, but somehow – because you are aware of that moment in time – you know (or hope) that the legs flying up in the air with all that soil are not yours.

Further percussions signified that this was a very successful attack, and you wish and hope that you are going to survive, but almost accept death as inevitable in this split-second thought-pattern.

The aircraft flew on as piles of ammo cooked-off; 45 Commando's Milan ammo was in helicopter nets awaiting a lift to the forward troops. These also cooked-off, sending lethal firework displays across the BMA. A 'cook-off' is when the heat or explosion of the original shell or bomb causes secondary explosions on the ground, in this case ammunition stored out in the open. These piles of ammo were about 75 metres apart, but an explosion on one pile seemed to set off other piles nearby, sending further shrapnel and rockets all around the BMA.

Before we emerged from the relative safety of the lowest point in our trench, some brave, switched-on people were already organizing, getting things moving, treating the wounded and checking to see if the body, with no legs, was really dead or not.

Marines were stunned but were able to follow simple orders amongst the carnage. Gradually, people switched on and started using their initiative. Then, the intense medical training given to us on the sail down to the Falklands kicked in. Pressure was applied to wounds, triage steps were quickly activated, lives were saved and conditions stabilized. Morphine was given and the screaming quietened down to a dull moaning.

The sergeant major was carried off to the medical centre with serious wounds. This was a person whom we all looked up to and relied upon, but he couldn't help it; he looked bad and we feared he may die.

The body that nobody had even gone near, with the spine ripped out of the back, was obviously dead and lying on a trench side, and was finally looked at after the living had been treated.

This was mainly for identification purposes, as people were missing and maybe buried or vaporized by the bombs. Limbs and flesh scattered in the blink of an eye. This is the reality of the phrase 'missing in action'. Unfamiliar faces were ashen grey and expressionless as they went about their business. You were aware that you too may have the same expression. There were feeble smiles of reassurance and offers of cigarettes or warm Rolos from deep pockets as some semblance of normality began to return. Soon, communication was once again established between living beings.

Steve turned the body over. 'Oh my God, it's George.'

We had all ignored one of our best friends. In fact, we had passed him by several times whilst treating others. We had all written the body off with just a glance.

We were no longer young and immortal. A bright light had gone out and the world was worse for it.

Seven were killed in this raid, and dozens more were seriously wounded and disabled for life.

HELICOPTERS DOWN

On the morning of the landings, 42 Commando was the reserve unit. Kept on board *Canberra*, the idea was that we could be landed quickly anywhere there was a problem. We spent the morning watching helicopters buzzing around between air raids, anticipating getting sent out at a moment's notice.

Gazelle helicopters are small, easily recognizable machines with a two-man crew. These were at first used to fly forward of the front-line troops and to spot where the enemy may be, with the intention of calling in naval gunfire or an air strike. And so it was that two Gazelles from 3 Commando Brigade Air Squadron flew up San Carlos Water, where it was reported that a company of Argies may be located.

On a beautiful clear day with light skies, they flew around a headland straight into the enemy company. One Gazelle was promptly shot down and hit a nearby hillside, killing both crew members. The other helicopter was hit and crash-landed in San Carlos Water Sound; the pilot was mortally wounded. The sergeant observer was able to free the pilot and himself from the sinking wreckage and started swimming for the opposite shore, towards the Argies, dragging his friend with him.

Before they retreated, the Argies opened up on the two struggling figures in the water, causing additional wounds to the pilot. The sergeant was able to swim ashore using the lifesaving technique of dragging his friend behind him. He later received a well-deserved bravery medal for his actions that day. They were picked up by landing craft a short while later and transported back to *Canberra*, the closest ship with medical facilities on board.

I can still recall the look on the sergeant's face as he was led away by a medical orderly. His pilot and friend was left covered in a white, blood-soaked blanket in the bottom of the landing craft. As he was helped past us and other observers on his way to the sick bay, I recognized the sergeant as one of the troop sergeants who had been in 45 Commando at the same time as me. He was a man who oozed confidence and seemed to know all there was to know about life as a Royal Marine, a truly professional sergeant with a cheery outlook on life. Yet here he was a white-faced, broken man, shoulders hunched forward in total shock and being shepherded along by a medical orderly.

I looked at Neil, but neither of us spoke, both of us thinking, 'If that's the effect that a short exposure to battle can have on a man like him, how am I going to cope when the bullets start flying around my ears?'

MOUNT HARRIET

The Unit Citation reads:

'On the night of 11/12 June 1982, as part of a night attack by 3 Commando Brigade Royal Marines to break into the Argentine positions defending Port Stanley in the Falkland Islands, 42 Commando Royal Marines assaulted and captured the key Argentine position on Mount Harriet. This night attack by 42 Commando Royal Marines had been preceded by 9 days of intensive and brilliantly conducted night patrolling over very rough ground, extensive minefields and in adverse weather conditions.

'The information acquired so painstakingly by the Commando's patrols was sufficiently detailed to enable the Commanding officer to make a bold plan to outflank the enemy positions and assault them from the rear. This attack from an unexpected direction aimed to catch the enemy, consisting of the best part of 4th Argentine Infantry Regiment and the Regimental Headquarters, by surprise. Furthermore, it would avoid a frontal assault through the main minefield and the enemy's planned killing ground.

'After a long approach march, the assault started about 2 hours after midnight. K Company, the leading Company got within 150 metres of the enemy before being fired on. The battle was on; the fighting was fierce. Bold and decisive leadership, combined with great aggressiveness, established K Company on the crest of the feature and then the long process of winkling out the enemy began. L Company then began their clearing operation through the heavily defended Western end of the enemy position. Meanwhile, J Company, who had diverted the enemy's attention before the attack, began supporting K and L Companies onto their objective.

'Despite the stubborn resistance by the enemy machine gunners and the enemy defensive artillery fire on the objective, the attack by 42 Commando Royal Marines was a brilliant success. The battle was fought with great dash and determination by the Commando, many of whom were suffering from cold injuries sustained in the preceding 10 days of appalling weather on Mount Kent and Mount Challenger. For the loss of two killed and 26 wounded, the Commando secured this vital feature; killing at least 50 of the enemy and taking over 300 prisoners, including the Regimental Commanding Officer and great quantities of equipment.

'For this great feat of arms, the Commando was awarded the following decorations.

One Distinguished Service Order
One Military Cross
Four Military Medals
Eight Mention in Despatches
One OBE
One MBE'

CASUALTIES OF WAR – IT'S A STATE OF MIND AND NOT A DUELLING SCAR

I once read that the Falklands campaign was the first conflict in history during which, as a ratio, more people were killed or wounded in actual fighting than died from disease or starvation. This was down to a number of factors, including the isolation of the battlefields from the civilian population and the swift decisive actions that took place. In all previous conflicts, the civilian population has been heavily involved, either directly, as in the Second World War, or indirectly through the spread of disease through bad sanitation or starvation, the breadwinners thus being wiped out or crippled.

At Agincourt in 1415, men considered it a glorious action and hoped that, if in the fray they were to get wounded, a neat duelling scar on the left or right cheek would suffice. They didn't imagine that their small slashing wound would fester and turn into sepsis, and that they would die in some foreign country, abandoned and in pain, as the army marched on.

As the all-too-optimistic Light Brigade charged the Russian guns in Crimea, 'death or glory' was the motto of the cavalry regiments that took part in the attack. No one considered that their balls might get blown off and that they would have to return home without the family jewels; or that whilst being treated in hospital for a shrapnel wound, typhoid would set in and wipe out more soldiers than all the Russian guns put together. Again, if lucky enough to survive, a small duelling scar would look quite dashing in the favourite haunts of young gentlemen and ladies back in London.

D-Day was a glorious action when viewed from a wider perspective, especially if the viewer was not there. All the units on D-Day achieved success on the first day, and some achieved their objectives. 47 Commando Royal Marines landed at Arromanches, having lost most of their support weapons and half of the fighting unit, along with the CO. They regrouped and marched off, picking up discarded German weapons as they went, and successfully attacked Port-en-Bessin the following day. This small town was vital for the link-up with the Americans on Omaha Beach, and would also be the place where the PLUTO pipeline across the Channel to fuel the Allied advance came ashore.

Complete success was achieved, but I bet if you were a member of that unit it felt like a disaster: losing 50 per cent of your unit on the first day when you had trained for nearly four years and become friends with many of the young men now wounded or killed in action.

47 Commando continued to fight on across France until withdrawn for another equally challenging amphibious assault on Walcheren Island, Holland, in November 1944. This assault by Canadian forces and a Commando brigade opened up the port of Antwerp to shipping and the logistics essential for advancing the Allied armies into Germany, helping to end the war in Europe. What unimaginable casualty figures these were!

By this stage, most people were aware of the nature of modern warfare, but alongside the advances in medicine that meant you were more likely to survive a battlefield wound came advances in weaponry, which meant the wounds were worse and more plentiful.

I think it was with this grim determination most of us set foot on the Falklands. We had a 'fingers crossed it won't be me' attitude; the same attitude that 50 per cent of 47 Commando had as their landing craft neared the D-Day beaches.

Most of the marines and paras had been to Northern Ireland or were expecting to go soon, so active service was accepted as part of joining up. Both regiments have a Corps history that has involved bloody conflict around the entire globe.

Every ten years or so since the Second World War, the Corps had been involved in one conflict or another: Korea, Suez, Aden, Borneo, Malaya, Northern Ireland. It was not a surprise that sometime in my career, bullets would be flying around my ears. I just hoped that they wouldn't be flying between them.

Nobody wanted to die on those remote islands some 8,000 miles away from home. From our time in Ireland, we knew it fucking hurt if you got wounded, so that wasn't something to look forward to either. Neither were duelling scars looked upon as a fashion accessory. I intended to stick to the 'I'm me and nothing could happen to me' approach.

I was more fortunate than most and didn't get involved in any of that nasty hand-to-hand fighting that the public and press imagine happens on every square inch of a battlefield. But some fantastic stories of courage and comradeship did come out of every unit that took part in these battles, and they are widely reported on in many books by the combatants, who have a right to spin these stories as their own experiences.

One such story involved K Company, 42 Commando, during the assault on Mount Harriet. During artillery stomps, the company commander was called over to a group of marines taking cover.

'Sir you have got to see this. Sergeant Paine has been wounded and has got three arseholes.'

Captain Babbington crawled over, feeling unnecessarily distracted from the battle that he was trying to command. Around Sergeant Paine was a group of marines with tears rolling down their cheeks from laughing at this poor unfortunate, who had his trousers down while someone tried to give him first aid between artillery rounds landing.

Paine had been hit by shrapnel in the cheeks of his buttocks – twice. The resulting wounds had the appearance of the only hole that was supposed to be there. The whole Company HQ joined in, which only became louder as Sergeant Paine realized that no one was taking his wound seriously.

A small duelling scar would not have got this reaction.

Paine had been a part of Bill's training team at Lympstone in 1977, one of those corporals who took his role a bit too far, and certainly without humour. In fact, Bill said he was a right bastard in training. Maybe this had assisted in bringing Bill's squad up to standard, but whatever the case, his behaviour was still remembered with bitterness by Bill. We met Paine in a bar in Exmouth about a year after the Falklands. He said hello and at first we spoke to him in stilted tones, especially Bill.

As the beer flowed, however, he started to speak politely to Bill, but in a guarded manner, as if he knew of his poor reputation with ex-recruits. Bill found himself lost for words at first, but decided to pipe up with a helpful, 'How is your arse now? Do your jeans still fit?'

An awkward silence moved like a slow-moving wave from the point where Bill had made his comment. We then all started to laugh, and Sergeant Paine even joined, remarking how difficult it was to sit on a bar stool with only one buttock. He added that he was looking at getting a boob job for his arse.

'That would make you feel a right tit, I expect,' someone quipped helpfully. And on the evening went.

Not quite a duelling scar!

CENTRE ISLAND

C orporal 'Bish' Bishop had just about had enough. He had been due to 'go outside' and leave the Corps in May 1982. He had a twenty-two-year pension and a cushy civvy job lined up, and was in the process of carrying out his extended leaving routine when the CO had cancelled all leave and all drafting, including blokes due to 'go outside'. Bish was seen to have essential skills, as he was fully trained and experienced in the Motor Transport Section, in particular how to waterproof vehicles and prepare helicopter landing sites.

Bish had been sent 'down south' in one of the Landing Ship Logistics. These were flat-bottomed ships that would carry all the unit wheeled vehicles, mainly the over-snow BV's which were considered to be best for the terrain of the Falklands, although some Land Rovers with signals equipment were loaded as well. They were all going to be airlifted off by helicopter.

Bish had been detailed off to crew the LSL *Sir Percival*. When this ship had sailed into Falklands Sounds on the first day of the landings, it had been attacked by Argentine aircraft and been hit by two 500lb bombs. Fortunately, they had been dropped too low to go off, but unfortunately for Bish, they had entered the side of the ship and gone into the marines' mess deck, and one had demolished Bish's locker with all his kit inside.

The ship was evacuated, and bomb disposal teams had gone in amongst where the bomb was, cutting lockers and kit to get at it, liberally spreading seawater and oil all over the place. The ship was saved, but Bish was left without his kit.

Whilst ashore, Bish, being an old hand, was able to meet up with mates from the stores departments and get more kit issued. He was, however, unable to get a Bergen in which to put it all, so he took to carrying around his newly proffed kit in a black poly bag. He was caught up in another air raid whilst waiting for the bomb to be defused on the *Percival*. Bish leapt into a crowded trench just before two 1,000lb bombs landed amongst the ammunition of the Brigade Maintenance Area. He came out of the trench deafened by the explosions and started to assist in the clear-up operation. Bish knew that it was of little strategic or tactical importance, but was bloody annoyed to see that his black poly bag had been shredded by the explosion, with what was left of his kit having been spread all over the BMA area.

Once again, he called in some favours and got his kit reissued just before he was tasked to get on the *Sir Galahad* with a small team of marines and assist in the off-loading of the heavy equipment of the Welsh Guards in Bluff Cove.

Two days later, Bish found himself wandering along a barren shore, deaf and kitless yet again, as he watched the bombing and burning of *Sir Galahad* just off the beach. This time he had also lost his rifle in the blackened hold of a ship. Again, there was no way he was going to make a fuss. Around fifty men had just died, and many more were seriously injured, while he had escaped yet again by the skin of his teeth. Besides, there was too much to do, assisting with the casualty evacuation and setting up helicopter sites to take the more severely wounded to the BMA. This process carried on all day. Towards the end of the process, those left standing around uninjured but stunned just used their initiative and tagged onto another unit.

Now that he was without his kit or a ship, Bish once more decided to rejoin his unit, jumping on a helicopter to 42 Commando's rear location at Teal Inlet.

Bish, a well-liked and respected old hand, told the blokes in the rear echelon of his adventures. I think we all knew that he was underplaying his part in the rescue operation, which he did by putting an amusing spin on the amount of kit that he had lost so far and the close scrapes that he had endured. The Quarter Master (QM) put him to use in the stores department, forwarding replacement kit to the front-line troops.

'If we get any more air raids, then fuck off away from the stores, Bish. With your luck, the Argies will get a direct hit and write off 42 Commando's logistics backup, and then we will all be fucked,' the QM told Bish whilst he was picking up his Bergen and kit and leaving Teal Inlet on the next available helicopter to make his way forward to the front line and action in the mountains.

Maybe the QM, with twenty-five years of service, and this being his first real war, wanted to lead a company into battle, and thinking that Bish was a 'Jonah', decided that he would take his chances with the incoming artillery shells at the front. Who knows, but we didn't see the QM again until after the surrender, as he placed himself in the 'safer' front-line area away from Bish.

Bish was soon fully equipped once again with a new Bergen and kit, plus a submachine gun that had belonged to a casualty who had been transported onto a hospital ship. He was particularly pleased with getting a new sleeping bag issued by the stores Colour Sergeant. These bags were made of a lighter, warmer material than the traditional feather-down-lined bags. The only thing that caused a raised eyebrow was that it was bright orange on the inside; not the best tactical colour, but beggars can't be choosers. Bish was chuffed that he would be warmer, but was concerned that maybe he had just been issued with the world's brightest aiming mark.

Bish joined in with all the rear-echelon activities, stores parties and helicopter under-slung loads. Incoming casualties were offloaded and stretchered off to the nearby Dressing Station. Ammunition and water were forwarded to the front line. He stopped bothering to wear ear defenders whilst working with the helicopters. He said there seemed little point as he had gone deaf anyway, and at any moment some Argie jet was more than likely going to heave a pair of 1,000lb bombs near to his vicinity, causing him further and permanent hearing loss.

One afternoon, the sergeant major gathered together all available ranks and gave us an update. We heard the sorry news of all the Welsh Guardsmen on the *Galahad*. Bish had not gone into detail when relating his experience on board when the *Galahad* had been bombed, but one could only guess at the horror of it all. As tragic as the disaster at Bluff Cove was, it did focus the overall strategy on getting on with the war. 42 Commando, 45 Commando and 3 Para were waiting patiently in the mountains, carrying out patrol after patrol, night after freezing night, with a view that the Guards would be carrying out some of the night attacks too. Now that the Welsh Guards had become operationally ineffective, it meant that other plans could be actioned.

During this briefing, the sergeant major mentioned that he wanted four volunteers to take over an observation point (OP) that the SBS had been operating on Centre Island since before the landings. It had been a forward operating base, but a presence had to be maintained there to spot any mining actions at the Teal Inlet entrance, either by aircraft or naval vessels.

'Fuck that,' Bill muttered under his breath. 'Shitting in plastic bags for a week and no fucking back up, I'm not volunteering for fuck all.'

'What's that, Bill, did you say? You're volunteering. Well done lad, how about you, Bish, say something if you don't want to play as well?' Bish stood there motionless, trying to lip-read.

Using these tactics, the sergeant major soon had a party of 'willing volunteers'. The other half of the party was recruited using more traditional methods, and three young, green marines also put their hands up, thinking only of the excitement of doing some essential real-life Special Forces SBS role.

'What the fuck did you put your hand up for, Lew? You could have taken my place instead, you twat,' Bill remarked angrily out of the corner of his mouth to me.

Bish stood around looking confused, with his jaw dropped and mouth open in order to pick up what was to him a dull-defused-monotone sound coming from the sergeant major's mouth. He had been in the service long enough to realize from the sergeant major's smile and body language that he too had just been detailed off for another shit job.

A rigid raider was used to transport the 'willing' bunch of volunteers. These are 18ft, open speedboats with very powerful engines and little to keep you dry. The cox'n of these craft only seem to know two speeds – stop and full speed. The stopping is no doubt a trained skill and generally involves sending up a great wash onto any shore or moored craft nearby. Slowing down gradually on approach was obviously not part of the landing craft course. The full-speed bit was essential too; there could, after all, have been an ITN camera crew on the shore filming another raiding party setting out to do daring deeds and beat up the enemy. If some cameraman had captured the party setting out, it would at least have to look the part; camouflaged faces, bristling with weapons, consisting mainly of machine guns proffed from Argie prisoners, and piles of specialist stores.

The truth was that an old deaf corporal was leading a scratch bunch of green marines and complaining, dripping old sweats to some remote island, where the main task of the operation was to free up the SBS for other more important action. As we headed off, we had pockets full of plastic bags to defecate in for a few days and the best rations of any troops on the Falklands, freshly proffed from the QM's stores. The machine guns and ammo were only being taken along for overwhelming firepower in the defensive role in case we were attacked. We had no plans to assault Port Stanley in a rigid raider.

Needless to say, the rigid raider cox'n stayed dry on his 30-knot speed trip across the Sound, whilst the rest of us got soaked as cold South Atlantic waves crashed over the bow of the vessel, leaving all of the weapons and most of our kit wringing wet. Fortunately, I had packed my Bergen with two black poly bags as waterproofing, so my sleeping bag stayed dry. Some were not so lucky, and the thought of a few days and nights on a cold, exposed island while fighting off hypothermia was too much for Bish.

Upon arrival, the landing craft carried out a very rare silent approach. No doubt the cox'n was trying to impress the SBS OP on the island and didn't want to be filled in by some Special Forces sergeant for compromising his position.

Bish was having none of it. He had wrapped his hand in (Royal Marine speak for having given up) at last. He got a quick briefing from the SBS sergeant, who seemed annoyed that he had to repeat everything twice in a loud voice. The SBS party who had been on the island in hides for two weeks, shitting in plastic bags and eating cold rations so as not to give their position away, then moved cautiously and tactically towards the waiting landing craft.

The cox'n stood by, just itching to impress the SBS that his craft could still move along at 35 knots despite the heavy swell in the Sound. He seemed oblivious that this would also predictably throw giant waves into the seating area of the boat and all over the passengers.

As all thoughts of a covert exit were dismissed and full throttle was engaged, the SBS lads hung on to anything solid that they could. They gave a last wave whilst staring incredulously at Bish as he turned his sleeping bag inside out and lay the bright orange, soaking wet material to dry on a low gorse bush, in full view of any passing enemy aircraft or patrol, whilst humming 'We'll hang out the washing on the Siegfried Line' at the top of his voice!

WOODEN CROSSES

A request was sent out from Commando Logistics Medical Squadron for us all to donate another pint of blood due to the high number of casualties coming in from the various mountain battlefields. We had already given a pint on the *Canberra* about a month before. Lads had queued up on the *Canberra* and made comments such as, 'I hope you're going to put my name on that bag in case I need it later.'

A month later, I found myself again standing in a queue waiting to go into the dressing station at Teal Inlet to give another pint of blood. This time no jokes were made. Lying outside the same set of tents and right next to the entrance was a row of three laid-out Army blankets. Under the blankets were obviously the dead bodies of British soldiers. I could see the DMS boots and puttees sticking out of the bottom of the blankets, feet at a 45-degree angle. One of the blankets had a large fresh blood stain around the head area. Whilst in the queue, the medics carried out another body on a stretcher and gently placed it in a grassy area. This one had the same boots on as I was wearing, so was most likely a Royal Marine.

I thought, 'That could be me or one of my friends under one of those blankets.' All were young men with Mums or wives about to get a visit from a padre and senior officer at home.

Once I got past the first visual shock of this, I began to wonder if this was the right place to lay out dead bodies. However, as I entered the dressing station, where surgeons and other medical staff were working flat out on the steady stream of wounded coming in from the mountain battles, I knew it was just a practical necessity. The area inside the tents was for the living and those whose lives could be saved. All the space was required, as there were so many British and Argentinian casualties. Those outside were in no rush to go anywhere and could be shown greater respect later, when the steady stream of helicopters stopped landing on the LZMT.

I asked one of the 42 Commando medics, who was setting up the bag to take my blood, if it was OK to take another pint of blood when I had just given one a month ago. 'Yeah, you'll be fine, Lew,' he replied. 'You are fit and healthy, just make sure you drink and eat enough. Your body will soon replace it. If you feel like you're going to faint, just lie down.'

We both looked up as a couple of stretcher-bearers carried in an Argentinian captain, who was in shock with a wound to his shoulder but was sitting up and looking around at all the amazing medical activity going on.

'Hello, Sir,' said my medic. 'We will put you down there for now and get you into the doctor as soon as possible.'

'OK, thank you,' he replied quietly in perfect English.

'If you are O Positive, like Lew here, we could just connect you straight up together Sir,' my medic offered helpfully.

'Ah, OK,' he murmured. The large 'M' written on his forehead in brown cam cream indicated that he had been given a syrette of morphine by a British front-line medic when he had been treated on the battlefield for his shoulder wound. This, together with the shock of his injury and capture, explained why this obviously capable company commander was so subdued.

'OK, Lew, that's you drained. Next please,' my medic said cheerfully.

As the death toll mounted, a feeling spread through the company of wanting to do something more for these poor young men whose lives had ended so suddenly and violently. The living and wounded could be evacuated onto hospital ships; but the dead? What was going to happen to them? Repatriated home in some refrigeration ship? Buried at sea?

We had attended the burial at sea of the two helicopter crew from the *Canberra* on the first night of the landings. That was sobering enough, but here there were now twenty-eight dead paras and marines who needed to be treated with respect and care so that something more permanent could be organized later on.

There must be people in the military machine who are briefed on how to deal with mass deaths on a battlefield. I was aware that one of the many roles of a sergeant major in conflict was to leave one dog tag with the body and take the other one for records, but that was about as far as it goes. Maybe they cover that on the WO2 course?

My concerns were answered two days later when twenty-eight body bags were laid out in a mass grave dug by bulldozers at Teal Inlet. Everyone available stood in neat ranks, berets off, listening to the padre's funeral sermon as General Moore and his staff stood in the large dug-out grave, saluting the row of prone body bags. The Royal Marine bugler did not drop a single note of the Last Post at the end of the service.

We right-turned on command and walked off, very much moved by the service and the efforts that had been made to give the best send-off possible in the demanding circumstances.

Afterwards, we sat around in one of the sheep-shearing sheds having a wet of tea and contemplated what we had just witnessed.

'I expect the Commonwealth War Graves Commission will arrange crosses for the graves of those who are not sent back to the UK,' Joe remarked.

'That will take ages,' Jim commented.

'Do you reckon you and Lew could make some crosses? There is a timber store in one of the sheds at Teal Inlet,' Jim enquired of Sergeant Les Limburn, my boss.

A small team of us set about selecting the best wood from the timber store and started to construct simple wooden crosses using hand tools from my carpenter tool kit, which had finally caught up with our Echelon, along with many other much-needed stores and weapon spares. These would have been very useful four weeks ago, but had instead stayed on the *Canberra* and completed the long voyage to South Georgia and back across the South Atlantic.

The armourers used black rifle paint to neatly paint the name, rank and number of the fallen onto the crosses. When a minor mistake was made, such as a fault in the timber or joint or a name not spelt exactly right, we binned that cross and started again. Over the next two days, our team of elves gradually completed their cathartic task, and the graves, which were now filled in and turfed over, formed a large Anglo-Saxon-like burial mound, similar to the ship-shaped mound at Sutton Hoo in Suffolk. These were now topped off with twenty-eight neat wooden crosses.

I traced the names on the crosses of each person I had known with my index finger and returned to my tent, falling asleep once the shivering stopped.

WHITE FLAGS FLYING OVER PORT STANLEY

We moved off the mountains and a handful of other locations and into Stanley, the capital 'city' of the Falklands. Some yomped, some got lifts in helicopters, and 42 Commando came back together again as a unit at Moody Brook, the old Naval Party 8901 Royal Marine Barracks. The place was a shambles. I think we had shelled it with 105mm artillery and sent the last of the Argies packing.

The Argentinians had also left the place in a mess, literally shit all over the place where they had no discipline over sanitary arrangements. Looted NP 8901 stores and live ammunition were scattered all around. Someone found a Royal Marines dress pith helmet with a fresh turd inside it; we laughed and put that down to 2 Para, who had yomped past that way earlier in the day. Another clue was the note inside, where someone had scribbled and spelt Parachute as 'Parashute' when leaving the greeting.

We could appreciate the subtle sense of humour engaged by those witty pongos and would have returned the favour given the chance. No doubt they were all euphoric, having just survived a campaign which far outweighed anything they had been involved in at the pubs of Aldershot. (Pongo is a nickname for the British Army – where the army goes, the pongos!) Paras are of course a bit special; they jump out of perfectly good aeroplanes with parachutes, but when they hit the deck they become pongos.

Of course, there is regimental rivalry between the Paras and Royal Marines, but most enlightened folk consider this healthy as it keeps up the high standards essential for elite and effective front-line troops.

There is a true admiration and comradeship between paras and marines which is enhanced further in combined operations. I recall the sheer determination and efforts on the faces of the superb 2 Para soldiers as they made their way through our positions on the way to their second and most successful battalion attack on Wireless Ridge. Heads up, alert, looking around, faces creased with the sheer human effort of carrying large loads and the trepidation of what was about to befall them in the coming night's battle.

42 Commando had been warned prior to the Mount Harriet battle that they may be ordered to exploit further forward onto the Mount Tumbledown feature, but had been stood down as it was seen as being over-ambitious by the brigadier, 42 Commando having run out of both the cover of darkness and ammunition. The fresh and keen Scots Guards would capture that bit of history the following night.

So as 2 Para yomped past, they were observed with grudging admiration and comradely nods as the marines took what shelter they could in boulder-strewn rock runs, with soaked-through sleeping bags with crusty ice around both the boot and the head end, pulled up around unshaven teenage necks. They hungrily tucked into large tins of looted corned beef with greasy bent spoons whilst recharging magazines with the copious abandoned 7.62mm ammunition lying around the captured position, knowing that had the order been confirmed, they would have accepted their lot, picked up Bergen and rifle and headed off to their fate on Mount Tumbledown. However, the order did not come. So rest, recuperation and survival was the order for the next few hours, and all supportive wishes went from those wet, clinging sleeping bags, and the huddles of marines struggling to light a cigarette in the swirling near-gale conditions, to the men of 2 Para as they stumbled over scree slopes and made their way to their fate. No one knew when the conflict was going to end, but even a truce or unconditional surrender would not take away the mental threat of being in touching distance of injury or death.

The following morning, after a massive fireworks display on all the mountains around us, the lead elements of the Task Force witnessed the folding of the Argentinian forces around Stanley. 2 Para exploited forward from their successful night battle on Wireless Ridge, following up the retreating, stumbling, routed individuals who had escaped death, injury or surrender. Small olive-green hooded figures could be seen in the far distance, having abandoned their weapons while making for the outskirts of Port Stanley in the early morning light.

40 Commando were accidentally helicoptered forward further than they had expected due to a navigational error by the pilot, landing on Sapper Hill just outside Stanley. They were pleased to find a few Argies vying for a fight on their impromptu landing site.

Our signals sergeant had spent most of his time with two sets of headphones on, listening intently into any developments, and on occasion offered us detailed snippets of information. They were, however, hard to connect up to the bigger picture. I think that was why he always looked slightly baffled as he tried, forlornly, to continuously piece together this information through the background hiss of static and distorted speech.

That morning, though, he was decisive. He flung open the door of his signals tent and declared loudly, 'White flags have been seen flying over Stanley!' He added, 'Bloody marvellous!' He then froze, and a look of concentration came on his face as further messages came through. Back he went behind his tent flaps to carry on his vigil, not to be seen again until we moved off later that day. We all hugged and slapped each other's backs noiselessly with padded arms and double-gloved hands. I wondered if this was the 'really cold' that my troop officer was referring to in training.

Joint operations, in more recent conflicts such as Afghanistan and Iraq, have cemented far more effective cooperation and understanding of each other's role, which is essential to operate effectively on a modern battlefield.

The Paras have continued to set high and ambitious standards, but have transformed into a modern, super-effective air assault role with integral support, meaning that they can operate independently in any conflict.

The Royal Marines continue to transform on almost a six-monthly basis to take account of modern-day threats. They maintain the traditional amphibious and naval support roles, but these are only an element of what they do. Google the Royal Marines and you will see modern-day marines flying armed drones, using GPS for pinpoint accuracy on fire missions and navigation. Every marine is connected to each other and supports a range of arms from laser-guided missiles to the awesome Apache helicopter, which alone is conflict-changing.

The young men and women volunteering for the British armed forces today are mastering technology that wasn't even on the wish list in the 1980s. As the world changed, both regiments struggled to find new meaningful roles and gain funding, whilst desperately morphing to keep up. Both organizations required greater funding than a normal army battalion and could be seen as a swift method of cutting the defence budget if it was a choice between an 'Armoured Farmer' regiment (such as the East Anglian Regiment) and a Royal Marine Commando unit or Parachute Battalion. However, it is good that someone in Whitehall has made the correct decision and found a role for both regiments in the modern, meaner, leaner British Army.

However, in the Falklands in the 1980s, it was just a pleasure to have ferried the Paras down 'south' in Royal Navy ships and then landed them safely ashore with Royal Marine landing craft. They became an integral part of the 3 Commando Brigade under Royal Marine command, supplied by the Royal Marine Logistics Regiment and supported by 29 and 59 Commando Artillery and Engineers. Helicopters from Royal Marines Air Squadron transported them forward and brought their wounded back to Royal Marines Medical Squadron field hospitals.

2 and 3 Para certainly punched above their weight in the Falklands War. With state-of-the-art technology making effective helicopter assaults the norm, I for one am convinced that throwing pongos out of the back of a Hercules is a thing of the past.

I think the QM had the last laugh, as he was one of the officers put in charge of the move back to the UK. The Paras got the flat-bottomed landing ships, in which they were seasick all the way back to Ascension Island. The Corps loaded onto the *Canberra*, the flagship of P&O. Oh, how we chuckled at the pith helmet incident as we steamed sedately past the storm-battered landing ships in a South Atlantic gale, at 23 knots on the way home, as they chugged along at a sedate 12 knots, bobbing around like corks.

After the Argentinian surrender, we had moved into our allocated shelter in Moody Brook, just outside Stanley, while some of the unit went into a hangar at the barracks and others went into a refrigeration plant. The roof and walls of the hangar we were in were peppered with small holes created by shrapnel from near misses and from bombs or shelling that had scythed through the thin tin plate. It was the first time in almost a month that we had a roof, of sorts, over our heads. We started to settle down and get organized, with any remaining Argie and NP 8901 stores immediately proffed. The Argies had left behind more large tins of corned beef and other unimaginable treasure! We must have been in the clothing stores, as when we sorted through large cardboard boxes, we found new clothing still in plastic bags. These were enthusiastically ripped open, like children at 4am on Christmas Day morning, to reveal new Argie green cotton T-shirts and underwear. We ditched our honking nicks and shirts, which had become crusty and U/S (unserviceable), and replaced them with good quality South American Gucci green long johns. Being near a refrigeration plant, we were also able to help ourselves to the large store of Argentinian beef. Blokes used jack knives and gollocks (large machetes) to cut prime joints from whole sides of beef, then fried them up in mess tins. It wasn't long before we even got chefs using abandoned Argie mobile kitchens to do some quite palatable meals for us. Of course, nobody told Taff the chef that he was doing a really valued job. He understood that blokes in long queues, stamping their feet against the cold and dripping about the T-bone steaks being overdone, and the syrup from the tinned peaches being too sweet, was actually just as complementary as any enthusiastic round of applause from the guests of a posh officers' mess dinner.

As we settled into our new accommodation, we were stunned that so many had survived, apparently unscathed, but saddened at the deaths and serious injuries of so many friends from around the Corps. Some were on hospital ships and in the process of being casevaced home. We didn't know how many of them would survive. The last time they were seen was with terrible wounds, being loaded onto helicopters, and we didn't get minute-by-minute updates; just 'Frank has been flown home via Accession Island and was last reported as stable' or '14 men were lost on HMS *Glamorgan* and loads got injured'. No meaningful updates were provided, because the technology and communications just did not exist.

The habit of giving everyone nicknames didn't help as the casualty lists were slowly published. Initially, you could read a casualty list and skim past the announcement that Marine Paul Scott Gardener was listed as KIA. Nowhere did it list 'Scotty' as KIA. We only found out later, during some catch-up conversation on the *Canberra* with an old mate from another unit, that it was actually Scotty who was dead.

We all just wanted to get home, by plane, ship or whatever. The preferred option was the *Canberra*, as all our spare personal kit and stores were still on board, stowed away for safekeeping. The thought of a cruise home through the equatorial regions, and feeling the warmth of the sun again on our skin, was also very appealing.

Cups of tea and being warm became luxuries in such conditions. One person who was taking full advantage of this was Marine Smith, the company commander's signaller. He had the job of being close at hand to the boss, a mature and forthright officer who didn't stand any messing around. Signallers generally spend their lives with a background hiss going on in their heads, due to the fact that they have an earpiece on one ear whilst the other end of the headset is perched on the top of their heads so they can at least hear something of the outside world. This sometimes leads to them talking too loudly or misunderstanding a message spoken to them from nearby.

During one incident near Mount Kent, the company snake (single line of following soldiers) was yomping along when the message was passed back: 'air raid warning red'.

This passed on down the line, and the Marines started scanning the sky and looking to the horizon in all directions. When the message got to Marine Smith (Smudge), he took a second to decipher the message against the background of the radio hiss and shouted out, 'What! The twat hasn't got us lost again has he?' With this, the company commander decked him.

Now, at the end of the conflict, Smudge had survived the company commander's short fuse, not to mention the fast enemy jets and artillery bombardments. He was inside a large shed and safe, standing with his back to the company commander whilst he spoke to someone on the linked handset plugged into Smudge's radio on his back. Smudge was still on listening watch, with his headset on one ear, oblivious to what was going on around him. He cupped his hands around a full pint of sweet pusser's tea in a black plastic water bottle mug. He was warm and dry in his newly acquired Gucci green long johns and was looking forward to getting back on the ship for a long hot shower and a beer. Life was good.

The company commander called one of the troop sergeants across. 'Sergeant Harmer, we haven't got enough space for Company HQ in here. Can you move some of your troop into here and we will go into the space that your troop are in.'

Very rarely did I see NCOs and officers clash face to face, particularly in front of the men. However, these two had been at each other's throats throughout the campaign. The sergeant, with some justification, thought the company commander was crap at map reading. Several times whilst yomping around the Falklands, he got us 'slightly' lost. Sergeant Harmer had corrected him several times without fuss, despite Marine Suggs's helpful comments.

'Fuck off, Sir,' Harmer replied. 'We've got more in the troop than Company HQ and they won't all fit in there.'

The company commander, taken slightly aback by this outspoken resistance, retaliated more forcefully.

'Sergeant Harmer, we've got twelve in Company HQ, that's almost half a troop.'

'Name them then, Sir. Go on, name them,' Harmer challenged in a louder tone.

Marines sitting around cleaning their rifles and talking amongst themselves looked up.

The boss spluttered, 'We've got about twelve, there's Marine Smith, the Company 2i/c, the company clerk, the CSM and uh, uh.'

'That's not twelve; go on, name another eight,' Harmer announced triumphantly, now aware that he had an audience.

'Well, there's, there's, uh. Oh, bollocks to this!'

With that, he punched Sergeant Harmer squarely on the chin. Harmer fell back, well and truly decked, but bounced up again as if he had hit a trampoline. He landed a haymaker right on the company commander, taking him down and to his right, and a grappling match ensued.

Totally oblivious of the build-up, Marine Smith was suddenly jerked backwards into the affray by the lead still connected to the radio on his back, his full black mug of hot pusser's tea spilling all over the front of his chest and face as he fell between the grappling pair. There was a look of horror on his face as if to say, 'I've survived the war, but I am just about to be beaten to death by the company commander!'

Marines leapt to their feet and shouted encouragement.

'Go on Sarge, fill him in', or 'Deck him, boss.'

Meanwhile, Smudge covered his head with his arms as best as he could as they rolled around and over him.

The other two troop sergeants broke it up, physically pulling the pair apart and standing in front of the large officer whilst the other sergeant held the arms of Sergeant Harmer.

The incident went no further. I think it was resolved by them not speaking to each other on the two-week passage home and a swift draft to Scotland for Harmer after summer leave.

Marine Smith, meanwhile, started to become more cautious. He would watch where he put his feet, as if there just might be an anti-personnel mine somewhere with his name on it, and also drank his tea with his back to the wall.

GINGE AND THE HAND GRENADES

The surrender came as a great relief to us all. Suddenly, the prospects of a longer life became a reality, and we all started to tread more carefully, ensuring that weapons were made ready and not fully loaded with a round up the spout. No point in getting shot in some stupid accident after all we'd been trough. I became more aware of how dangerous it was to fly in helicopters again; gravity was a serious threat, let alone pilot error or mechanical failure due to the overstretched machinery that had been flying constantly for over a month without correct maintenance schedules.

We had all crammed into the only Chinook helicopter left and flew to Moody Brook. Piled around were stores, Milan anti-tank rockets and marines with hand grenades hanging off their webbing. I ended up with my feet braced over the under-slung load doorway, my Bergen safely hooked into someone else's kit, preventing my arse from falling through the hole. I had a good view of the mountain tops as we skimmed our way across the barren rock features, which had been the scene of intense battles only forty-eight hours before. I was only too pleased to land safely at Moody Brook, which was located on the outskirts of Port Stanley, after the short but worrying flight. The unit was to reorganize at this base and wait for the next ship home – hopefully.

The sergeant major organized clearing parties to make the place safe and to tidy our area up. We were issued with ten Argie prisoners each, and using our best communication skills got them to clear up sewage, ammo and dumped equipment. 'Good NCO training,' the sergeant major told us with glee, as single marines marched their ten enemy soldiers forming the working parties into the nearby hills, with only a rifle and instructions to make sure they picked up all the crap.

Ginge, the ammo storeman, had the task of collecting all the unused primed grenades from the unit. These were considered a priority. Fused grenades of high explosive and white phosphorus were dangerous at the best of times, but they had now been fused for over a month and had been subject to all weather conditions, most had lost the paintwork and some had serious dents in them. Ginge arrived back at Moody Brook with a commandeered Argie pickup full of this sort of ammo. He parked it near the unit accommodation and went to get some tea.

'Who is the knobber who parked that truck near the accommodation with all those fucking grenades aboard?' the Quarter Master demanded.

All eyes looked at the ammo storeman.

'Ginge, get rid of those grenades ASAP!' the QM ordered.

Nearby was a huge great 1,000lb bomb crater that had been made in an air raid by a British Harrier. That seemed as good a place as any to dump the grenades. So Ginge and another helper started pulling pins and throwing live grenades into the crater, with subsequent loud satisfying explosions.

At this, the balloon went up; radios came to life, helicopters were launched and ships started to train their guns in the anchorage.

Ginge got one hell of a bollocking and was again told to get rid of the grenades, but not by letting them off. This time he threw them into the nearby estuary, into deep water and out of harm's way.

Six hours later, however, the tide was fully out, revealing hundreds of grenades on a mud bank, again too close for comfort for the QM.

'Ginge, get rid of those grenades! You are the ammo storeman, now do your job,' the QM shouted across the base.

Ginge spent the morning with his boots and socks off, wading in the thick mud and picking up grenades, accompanied by helpful hints from marines standing around drinking steaming tea from big pussers' mugs.

'Didn't the QM like the new ammo store, Ginge?'

'What a cushy number the QMs department has, they've even got time to go for a paddle.'

We soon cleared off when Ginge started lobbing muddy, live grenades on the bank near us. If we continued to wind him up, he may have taken one of the pins out; we were all treading very carefully. Rumours went around that later that day, an abandoned pickup truck full of muddy grenades was found near 2 Para's position.

Whilst waiting to embark, many went 'gisit' hunting. This traditional custom is a bit like proffing, except that when you have the abandoned equipment from an army of 11,000 men dumped in the hills nearby, it's just too tempting to try to find that unique memento to show the grandchildren; normally a large gun or officer's pistol. When marines came back with too much to carry home from their foray into the hills, others were heard to say, 'Got any gisits?'

During these trips, we also fired off hundreds of rounds from abandoned weapons and piles of ammo. We set up ranges of boots, tin mugs and ration packs, and shot the hell out of them. Normally, when you fire hundreds of rounds on a range, it takes hours to clean your weapon correctly. Here, we just unloaded the weapon and dumped it.

On one such trip, we found an intact Argie Huey helicopter that had landed on the hillside and been abandoned. Ginge found a .50 calibre machine gun nearby with stacks of ammo. Wary of booby traps, we screwed the barrel on and let Ginge have the first go. Ginge fired 200 rounds at the otherwise serviceable helicopter. This was too good a chance to waste, so we all reduced the helicopter to scrap. Yet again, the balloon went up. Unfortunately for Ginge, he was on the machine gun when one of our helicopters flew over to investigate. A nearby Rapier missile battery just over the next hill had reported machine-gun fire. Ginge had been putting rounds just over the unseen Rapier battery, whose crews were not happy about it.

We waved and walked away from Ginge, just in case the helicopter called in an air strike. All the way down the hill, we took the piss out of Ginge. Someone said that another stores party had sighted the Huey helicopter and that it had been accounted for and was going to be recovered. Ginge might have to explain to the QM why it was full of holes.

'That was not MOD property and I'm fucked if I am going to pay for it,' Ginge was heard to mumble as we trudged back, pockets and Bergens full of pistols and other gisits, bazookas over our shoulders, with ideas of hanging them over the fireplace at Mum's house or the local pub when we got home.

At the same time, others were re-equipping themselves with Argie kit. The Argentinians' high-leg boots were very well made, whilst we were still using boots and puttees. Their boots were waterproof, made from the finest Argentinian cattle hide. Some of us were lucky and got a new pair from the abandoned stores. Others, like Taff, had size 12 feet – apparently not a popular size in Latin America. Taff, determined to find a good pair of boots, was forced to look amongst the hills and abandoned positions, hoping to find someone's spare pair. Whilst on one such raiding party, someone found a large boot, and knowing Taff's predicament called him over. It was a perfect fit; Taff only had to find the other one now. Which he did, nearby, but upon picking it up he found it to be heavy and water-logged. Unfortunately, it was also foot-logged. We found the body nearby, minus boots and one leg. Not to be put off, Taff cut the laces and extracted the foot. Also a perfect fit. 'Cinderella will go to the ball,' he announced.

This was bad enough, but having seen our faces full of sickened glee, he picked up the foot and tried to make the toes move by pulling the tendons.

'It works with chicken legs,' he said, as he performed his party piece, the long-dead, cold white digits grasping at thin air.

HOMECOMING ON *CANBERRA*

At fairly short notice, we were helicoptered onto the *Canberra* in Falklands Sound. The decision had been taken to leave 5 Brigade behind, and that the Commando Brigade and Parachute Regiment attached units would go home first.

As we got off the helicopter, the usual efficiency of the P&O crew came into play. We were led to our cabins by helpful stewards and other members of the crew, who were only too pleased to welcome us back. They were slightly guarded in their speech toward us, maybe half-expecting that the experiences we had over the past months would have changed us into bloodthirsty Rambos. Neil summed it up nicely and put things in perspective for our helpful crew: 'We signed up for this stuff, you didn't. At least when we went ashore, we weren't in danger of getting sunk like you were for the past month.'

I think mutual respect was very much in evidence, the crew pulling out all the stops to make us as comfortable as possible. They laid on a steak dinner the first night we were aboard and proudly served up meals that they had held back especially for our return. We didn't have the heart to tell them that next to our sheep-shearing shed had been an abattoir full of sides of beef that our cooks had been helping themselves to and feeding us with for the last week or so. Their effort was appreciated, nonetheless.

The experience of getting into a hot blasting shower after a month without a proper wash was unique. The *Canberra* had efficient water processing systems for salt water, so the water was almost unlimited. I spent about ten minutes in the shower, but the strangest thing was that afterwards, once dressed in dry clean clothing, I still didn't feel completely clean. Neil mentioned this too, and we both surmised that we would only feel properly clean again when we put civvies on.

The ship made good speed at 23 knots, overtaking battered naval frigates on the way home that were limping along at 16 knots. The South Atlantic had really taken its toll on some of the ships, the rust-streaked marks on the hulls hiding serious mechanical and weapon systems damage that could have caused real problems if the conflict had gone on much longer. We carried out a resupply at sea with the RFA *Appleleaf*, taking on more fuel and, more importantly, beer. The *Canberra* had been drunk dry within two days of us getting back on board.

We continued to make good progress and spliced the main brace (a rum tot) for the birth of Prince William, then the following night had the best sod's opera that I experienced in my whole time in the Corps. A sod's opera is a series of sketches or songs written by marines, covering a wide variety of subjects, from taking the piss out of officers to singing songs the theme of which was taking the piss out of officers. Of course, all the officers were invited along and roared with laughter as individuals were singled out for a hard time and publicly ridiculed. There were so many potential acts that the entertainment sergeant had to hold auditions.

Gus and I carried off a sketch about the poor issue of kit based on the Monty Python 'Cheese Shop' sketch. The crowning moment was Moss Tombs singing 'We're all going on a pusser's holiday', to the tune of Cliff Richards' 'Summer Holiday'. Today, this would have been filmed and maybe put on YouTube, and Moss would have gained a record deal. But maybe we were all so drunk on alcohol, with the realization that we were alive and well while many others were not, to see any artistic faults in the performance.

As we approached the Equator, warnings were put out as to the seriousness of smuggling weapons into the UK. We were told in no uncertain terms that we were going on an extended eight-week leave period but could spend it in Portsmouth detention quarters if we were caught with any smuggled firearms. An amnesty was not seen as necessary, as the CO had already put this message across before we got on board. In any case, the Atlantic Ocean was big, deep and just outside. Marines took furtive walks along the promenade deck with black plastic bags that disappeared after short, contemplative scans out to sea.

Right: Mark in about week 12 of 35 weeks training.

Below: 2 Section on Kings Squad Week.

240A TROOP KING'S SQUAD

Passed for duty by
HRH The Prince Philip Duke of Edinburgh KG, PC, KT, OM, GBE,
Captain General Royal Marines

Above: 240A Troop Pass Out Parade. The ones that were left out of 60 who joined 240A troop!

Left: Artic Warfare Training with 45 Commando in Norway.

Above: Followed by sunbathing on a Mediterranean exercise.

Right: Deck Hockey – A violent sport!

Above: Working with The Yanks, Sardinia 1980.

Opposite above: Week 1 of training. September 1978. Some had already left on the train home! Mark is top row 7th from right.

Opposite below: The author on a ski tour.

To The South Atlantic 'Quick March' April 1982.

A helicopter deck being built onto The Canberra Cruise ship – The workmen sailed with us wielding all the way to Gibraltar.

Bill's 21st Birthday on the way 'Down South'.

Units took turns to use the pool. When it was 3 Para's turn after us we emptied loads of Trigger fish into the pool that the lads had caught. They didn't half get out quickly again!

War is Hell. A stopover at Ascension Island.

The Beach.

Landing craft practice.

Cross decking on to HMS Fearless the day before the landings at San Carlos.

The Canberra now looking rust streaked from weeks at sea.

San Carlos dug in.

San Carlos. By kind permission of 'Bill'.

A Sea King takes off from the Canberra's forward helo deck.

Air Raid Warning Red – San Carlos Anchorage.

RFA Resource. Ammunition ship with 'Big Nasties' onboard. – 'If this ship goes up you won't have to worry about The Falklands anymore'.

HMS Antelope having been bombed by Argie aircraft is towed into the anchorage and moored up.

Later that morning HMS Antelope burns and breaks up.

The Norland used to bring 2 Para down south.

HMS Antelope's back breaks and the sea rushes in which put the fires out.

It was stunning to witness a modern Royal Navy Ship sink in front of us. By kind permission of 'Bill'.

HMS Antelope disappears beneath the waves with HMS Fearless in the background. Both photos were taken through standard binoculars.

Above: We were circled by HMS Plymouth as protection. This ship had a string of 30mm cannon holes running from the waterline to the upper deck. She had also just been bombed and had been hit by four 1000Ib bombs which had all failed to explode. True grit.

Opposite above: LZMT (Landing Zone Military Transport) Teal Inlet and the only Chinook to survive the Atlantic Conveyor being hit by an Exocet missile. Maybe that's Menu D being flown forward to 3 Para.

Opposite below: Get away from that map Lewis you will get us lost!

Left: The author on Arctic training 1985.

Below: View out of a Seaking helicopter as L Company move forward (Mark Rudland)

Above: Neil with an Argentine .50 machine gun. Just to see if it still worked. Once he had loaded it he got Ginge to test it out and then Ginge was pushed to one side as we all had a go! This gun was taken back and is now on display at Bickliegh Barracks Plymouth. By kind permission of 'Bill'.

Right: Neil proving that the Argentinians were not running low on ammunition! By kind permission of 'Bill'.

Above: Testing out captured weapons after the surrender. No need to clean them afterwards just ditch them on a pile!

Opposite above: Ginge threw all the live grenades into Moody Brook. Then the tide went out. 'Ginge get rid of those grenades!' The QM shouted. Ginge took off his boots and socks and went paddling. By kind permission of 'Bill'.

Opposite below: Mark Rudland (an early selfie on Mt Harriet, Falklands Islands 1982).

The welcome back at Southampton. The whole of Southampton water was full of vessels. The shore was crammed with our families and well-wishers.

Some big cheers went up as some ladies gave us a treat and a super view!

Sentry duty.

The Russians never invaded whilst we protected the NATO Northen Flank.

Major Mike Norman (OC of NP8901 and then J Coy 42 Commando) takes the salute as us veterans march past Major Gen Vaux CB DSO.

RSM Chisnell BEM has a nice chat with the author on the 40th Falklands reunion at Bickleigh Barracks. The RSM was only 28 when we went 'Down South'. I commented that how young he was to have such responsibility. He replied that he and Colonel Vaux were amazed at the time how well we coped with it all being 17 – 18 and 19!

As we approached the Channel, more black plastic bags were seen to be falling over the side. Neil and I had a pair of 9mm pistols that we had taken from some Argie prisoners. What made them even more valuable was that stamped into the gun was 'Pistola 9mm Industria Argentina 1982'. These would make us a small fortune.

Nevertheless, we decided that it was too risky, even if we converted them, as was our intention. So, guiltily, we walked to the side of the ship, feeling that we must be the last ones to be dumping weapons over the side. We stood there looking around for anyone in authority, or worse, military police. As we stood at the rail looking out to sea, awaiting our chance, we saw an automatic Belgian FN rifle spinning down from the deck above and landing in the white wake of the ship. A moment later, some more unknown weapons in black plastic bags came fluttering past. Someone casually barged through double swing doors at the entrance to the promenade deck and hurled a bazooka over the rail; it went spinning down past eight decks until an almost un-noticeable splash marked its landing spot in the wake of the great ship. As the *Canberra* steamed up the English Channel, there was a deadly New York-style ticker tape parade with a small arsenal of weapons raining down on either side at intermittent intervals. We dumped the pistols and nonchalantly walked back to our cabin, feeling that our leave was now secure.

As we progressed up the Channel, we sailed quite slowly and close in to some headlands near Devon. We were due to dock in Southampton in the morning and were a little miffed that we couldn't steam ahead and just get home, but it had been decided to time our arrival for the morning. As dusk set in, we could see car headlights continuously flashing from car parks facing out to sea. This was a clue to what was in store for us.

Jeremy Hands, the reporter who had been with our unit, tried to have one over on us in his reply to a young marine's question about what sort of welcome we were going to have in Southampton. He said, 'No, the people back home have all but forgotten you by now. The press coverage of the war has been downgraded since the surrender.' Later, he did a live broadcast to the nation from the flight deck of the *Canberra*, smiling between takes and sharing jokes with us, knowing how he had wound us up earlier.

I got my face on the live ITN evening news, along with many others in the unit. I had always promised myself that if I ever had the chance for my fifteen minutes of fame, and it was filmed, I wouldn't wave and shout at the camera like some demented football fan behind the local TV reporter when the home side had won. Well, since it was only fifteen seconds of fame and we had just won a war, I shouted and waved with the rest of them!

Jeremy Hands triumphantly finished his report with the words, 'Jeremy Hands, somewhere in the North Atlantic.'

It was with this same triumphant mood that the RSM threw Jeremy Hands into the crowd for the live link to be cut, and Hands was stripped naked and held up in front of his own camera crew, 'bollocky buff', like some unit hunting trophy. The camera crew continued to film. No doubt this footage appeared at the ITN 'Christmas do outtakes' for a few years.

The following morning, we awoke to the announcement in the up-market style of P&O pursers that, 'Your gourmet breakfast is served, after which the ship will be docking at Southampton where I think someone has laid on a small surprise for you.'

We got up, all smiles, talking non-stop and giving each other shit over minor events like getting in the way in the corridor or taking too long at the sink and making lame jokes. This constant and routine ribbing was mixed with individual anticipation of seeing your family and friends again, going out or to the pub, dressing in normal clothes, eating Mum's cooking and seeing the English landscape and home.

We walked out onto the promenade deck and looked out over the Solent and could see nothing but small boats moving out of the early-morning mist. P&O ships came past, then turned and sailed alongside us, with people aboard all cheering. More boats joined the flotilla as we moved into Southampton Water. It was a beautiful sunny day, and many of the young women on board the boats were wearing just swimwear. At our encouragement, and with the sheer atmosphere of the event, some girls on nearby boats were persuaded to take off their bikini tops, to massive roars of approval from the young marines cramming the sides of the *Canberra*.

As the mist lifted further and we neared our berth in Southampton Water, we could not quite make out a strange movement onshore. Andy, whose home town was Southampton, indicated that the area we were looking at was a huge green park, only it was no longer green. As the ship got closer, we could see that the whole hillside and every available space on the docks were crammed with people, banners, streamers and balloons.

Helicopter flypasts took place, and royalty and other guests started landing on the flight deck. TV crews were everywhere. The UK public could not have given us a better welcome home; this was old-fashioned healthy patriotism at its best. Royal Marine bands played 'Rule Britannia' and 'God Save the Queen' repeatedly, as large sections of the crowd joined in.

We lined the promenade deck and wondered if our families were amongst the crowd, and if they were, how on earth would they find us. In my last letter home, I had played down this day and told my Mum not to bother attending as it was bound to focus on getting us straight onto coaches and back to Plymouth. I regretted this as I watched the first group of Royal Marines walking down the gangplank and being met by friends and relatives, and hugging their loved ones on the dockside. Eventually it was our turn, and we picked up our kit and made our way down the gangplank to a sea of faces, banners and cheering.

Ginge was walking in front of me and was suddenly grabbed and dragged off into the crowd by his girlfriend. I turned around and spoke to Bill: 'Ginge has been snatched. Did you see him get dragged off?'

'Billy', a voice nearby shrieked, and Bill was enveloped by his Mum and sister, and also hauled off into the crowd. If Customs were going to go through us like a dose of salts, they were going to have to contend with the lynching that would follow from the jubilant crowd, who were in no mood for bureaucracy. I continued my short journey towards the large reception hangar as more cries of recognition came from the crowd. Then I saw my brother, Stephen, in the sea of faces. At 6ft 1in tall, he stood head and shoulders over the packed crowd. Smiling and waving, I could see the concern on his face for his younger brother. He had seen the news articles and the TV footage of young men on stretchers with legs missing. Would I have changed in these few short months?

We greeted each other with joy, but also with a slight hesitation on his part. He and the nation had just spent the last three months on a crash TV course on the capabilities of modern warfare. Two weeks sunbathing and relaxing on the way back with 3,000 of your mates on board was probably the best therapy you could get. We were not a war-weary or shattered army. The mood was the opposite; we were the same smiling, happy-go-lucky bunch who set out three months before – relaxed, confident and sun-tanned.

Stephen led me through the crowd, where I met up with uncles, aunts, cousins, sisters and … my mum. What a delight! I was with my family, caring people; this was the real world, away from the male-dominated regimental life. We all stood grinning at each other. My cousins Julie and Helen had grown up a lot since I had last seen them, and I gained quite a few credibility points as the twins hugged me on either side, friends moving past with their families in tow, some winking at me and saying, 'Alright Lew', as they passed by.

Whilst onboard, we had been given the option of either going on a week's leave, then returning to camp to make the unit operational again stores-wise before going on an additional six weeks' leave, or we could go home to Plymouth for the night, spend two days sorting the kit out, and then go on eight weeks' leave. To a man, the unit voted for option two.

Coaches were leaving the docks at regular intervals for Plymouth, and we had a choice of which one to get on, but knew we had to be in camp for noon the following day. It was tempting to go home to Basingstoke, just 40 miles away, where my aunt lived for a party, but this would cause problems in covering the 180 miles to Plymouth the following morning. Knowing that in two days we would all meet up again, I spent about four wonderful hours with my family, then got on a coach and headed for Plymouth.

The celebrations were far from over, as all the way down to Plymouth, through the small villages and towns of Dorset, people lined the way. At traffic lights, pub landlords placed crates of beer on each coach. Drunken local girls got on the coach and travelled to the next town, kissing and embracing everyone on board. One girl got on the coach wearing only a Union Jack flag; she was a local girl who obviously liked the local pasties. Someone trapped off with her and she came all the way to Plymouth on the back seat with her newfound, and now not so sexually frustrated, friend.

We got back to Bickleigh Barracks to find that all our rooms were ready, and for the first time ever, someone had sorted out our bedding. However, we couldn't get access to our kit that had been left behind.

It had all been locked in a large room. We decided this was because they obviously thought that we were not coming back and it was to prevent looting.

We were desperate to go ashore, so Bill, being billeted in Jacko's room and knowing that Jacko had been on the rear party, broke into Jacko's locker. We helped ourselves to his civvies and within ten minutes of arriving back in Bickleigh, we were heading for the main gate. We walked past Jacko, who was the main gate sentry, greeting him with smiles as we paraded his Duran-Duran look 'New Wave' shirts and trousers past him. We waved as we stepped onto the same coach we had arrived on for the driver to take us into Plymouth on his way back to Southampton.

At the back of the bus snored a drunken but contented girl wrapped in a Union Jack flag.

FIRST NIGHT BACK

n the autumn of 1981, the club scene in Plymouth was getting quite nasty. More clubs were opening up and all had thugs as bouncers on the doors, and traditional pubs were being bought up and run by big business.

Young Royal Marines were turning to on a Monday morning sporting shiners and broken teeth, and it was getting noticed by the CSM as well as the company commander.

Most marines don't start fights whilst out having a few 'wets', but they have, in the finest traditions of the Corps, been known to finish them if needs be. There's no need to start a fight; you're stronger and fitter than your average civvy, with more mates, and probably have a lot more disposable income. What is there to prove by lumping some dingbat from a run-down local housing estate? Even the ugliest bloke can normally trap off in Plymouth, so the need to prove oneself in this area didn't exist either. The macho contest is just not an issue.

It was, however, an issue for the bouncers working at a particular nightclub. Young marines were walking into this club, and due to their haircuts were easily identifiable. Teams of bouncers then started fights with them and took great delight in knuckling drunken 18-year-olds, so long as they were on their own and the odds were in the bouncers' favour.

'What happened to you, McDonald?' the sergeant major would ask.

'Took a fall whilst out, Sir,' came the standard reply from the bruised marine.

'Did you win?'

'No, Sir, actually I got filled in.'

'In that case, put him on a charge, Sergeant.'

This occurred on many morning parades at barracks. To admit having a fight was one thing, but to lose was even worse.

Sergeants were despairing of the young generation of Royal Marines.

'You're Royal Marines, for fuck's sake. The civvies in Plymouth never filled us in when we were sprogs. What the fuck's going on?'

Questions were asked of the corporals by the sergeants, and of the sergeants by the sergeant majors.

Rumour had it that a group of older hands got organized and went down to the club one evening, walked straight in, filled the bouncers in and used a baseball bat to smash up the optics before moving through the club and out of the rear fire doors, across the Hoe and into darkness.

Unfortunately, it was the same night that the sergeant major was putting his master plan into action. This included using the Special Investigation Branch (SIB) in the club as observers to see what was really going on. When this fracas occurred, the SIB blokes tried to intervene and got filled in themselves.

The next day, it was all in the papers and visits were being made to all barracks to find the culprits. None were found, however, but all the clubs and pubs in Plymouth banned marines for the foreseeable future.

In other circumstances, this would have been a disaster, but we were going on Christmas leave soon, followed by a three-month trip to Norway. Things may have calmed down by then and big business might have overruled a few local landlords' concerns over their bouncers getting a few more lumps on their already lumpy heads.

What in fact followed the Norway deployment was a recall from Easter leave and another three months away as the Falklands campaign started.

It was against this background that we went ashore on our first night home. Were we still banned from all the pubs and clubs? Far from it; the first beer in each pub was free, and everybody was patting us on the backs and started buying us yet more beer. The managers of the clubs were touting for business outside – 'Free entry and first drink free lads. Well done! Welcome back!'

We were from their city and were their local Royal Marines, so they gave us a genuine welcome back home into their pubs and clubs and offered us the best hospitality they could.

Once we had downed a few beers, we were wondering whether there was a chance of any other locals offering us a welcome home present. We had not been near women for four months, while some who had been in mountain locations in Norway had not had a 'bag off' for over six months. I was on the second list, and my chin was dropping at the female forms surrounding me in such close proximity in the bars. Double beer goggles were on, and the world was a wonderful place. We felt like kids being given the keys to Willy Wonka's Chocolate Factory, only we were hoping that 'willy' would not be 'wonky' later on!

It's a bit of a tradition on a summer's evening to take a girl up to Plymouth Hoe, an area of grassland that forms a romantic location overlooking Plymouth Sound harbour. It's also right next to the main pubs and clubs, so very little effort has to go into herding some potential 'bag off' around this location. If a refusal at the first fence was quickly established, the option to break off and walk the short distance back to the pub was always there.

Some evenings, slim, T-shirt-wearing lads with short haircuts were seen leaving clubs in their droves, an arm around some willing but large conquest. Like prize heifers willingly heading towards the milking shed, they were subtly manoeuvred towards the Hoe, or more often than not led by the young marine. Small talk was established, the local country accent interspersed with loud laughter as clothing was fumbled with and attempts were made at undoing bras that would make a pair of bowling balls feel agoraphobic. The prize was carefully shepherded towards a suitable space in a shelter, or else a prime grazing area overlooking the harbour was carefully selected.

'Ere, manners, tits first,' was ordered loudly in a West Country accent and echoed around the steps and walls of the war memorial, then out to sea. Ships would alter course in the harbour, thinking that they were about to strike the lido wall, and roosting seagulls took off, squawking as if in mortal danger.

After further desperate seduction techniques, a more placatory tone would be murmured: 'OK, but warm yer 'ands first.'

Bill, Gus and I met up with three girls on holiday from Birmingham. From memory, they were all 'essence' (i.e., good-looking girls), however we never saw them in the morning. They knew that we had just arrived home, all our chat-up lines worked, they laughed with us, got drunk and were great fun to be with. We all left a club together and bundled into their car, Bill giving directions towards the Hoe. With six in the car, things were going to be a bit crowded, so I volunteered to show Siobhan the view of Plymouth Sound from the war memorial. We sat on the bench entwined, me with the greatest sense of urgency, whilst Siobhan giggled as the Ford Escort's suspension was put through its paces nearby. At one point, Gus appeared briefly, waving at us through the sunroof before diving back in and carrying on with his quest.

We could not have had a better first-night run ashore. The girls even offered us a lift back to Bickleigh Barracks, but we declined, determined to finish the night off with 'big eats' at KFC or a kebab. Maybe they were the welcoming party for members of many other battle-weary units or ship's companies that week whilst on their short holiday. That mattered not, and we were eternally grateful as we travelled back down Bickleigh Lane in a gratis taxi offered by the driver, who was only too keen to hear a few war stories and drop us off at the main gate, with kebab grease dripping down our grinning chins.

15 SECONDS MORE FAME

The following morning at Bickleigh Barracks, whilst carrying out the run ashore debrief, Neil arrived with a bundle of daily newspapers.

He opened up the paper, turning to the centre pages, where we all were staring out in a close-up picture on the deck of the *Canberra* as it docked alongside Southampton. We were all waving and smiling, about six of us. Bill was the only one who was just outside the frame. Neil later sent away for the original, which Bill was in. He was the only one not smiling, so we gave him stick for being such a grumpy-looking bastard; otherwise, he too would have had his fifteen seconds of fame. Bill put it down to being mesmerized by the girls showing off their tits on the boat alongside us!

After getting the unit's kit back together in record time, plus a few more runs ashore in Plymouth, we were sent on the fantasy eight weeks' leave.

I shared a lift home with my friend, Mark, in his battered Hillman Avenger. It had been left on Bickleigh Parade ground for about six months without being moved whilst we had been down south. Mark used to only buy old cars and run them into the ground, driving the 600-mile round trip home most weekends that he had off. I would share the driving and petrol with Mark, but I always ensured that I had enough money in my back pocket in case the car broke down, which seemed ever more likely due to the rusty bodywork outside and the black masking tape holding it together inside. With a pair of jump leads, it started the eighth time and off we went, four of us, with all our kit and 'proffed' Argie goodies piled into the boot.

Some serious war mementoes were amongst the kit in the boot – bayonets, Argie helmets with blood stains still on, boots, empty brass

Argie 155mm artillery cases plus some of our own kit. The back of the car was a regular army surplus store. The most hazardous bags contained our washing, all ready to load into Mum's washing machine when we got home.

As we got to the other side of London on the A12, we drove into a huge traffic jam. (This was before the M25 when there was much less traffic on the roads, and it was considered just a mild inconvenience to drive through central London.)

It was a police road check. The IRA had just murdered the Blues and Royals in Hyde Park in a bombing incident, and this was an armed check on suspicious vehicles that may contain members of the IRA active service unit.

Oh bugger, there goes our eight weeks' leave, I thought. Four young men in a battered old Avenger, with enough kit in the boot to carry out a small military coup on a South Sea island. How could we not get pulled apart in any search?

'I really hope none of you have any Argie guns in your kit, because we are right in the shit if you have,' Mark said.

'No, no,' we all assured our dutiful driver, who could see his leave going down the swanny. We got to the front of the queue, and a very nice WPC spoke to Mark whilst her colleagues in the background eyed us with menacing suspicion. She politely told us what the police road check was all about and asked us to open the boot. Now, if George had been here with us, he would have charmed her and most likely got her phone number too. But with a dagger-like shock, I realized that George had been gently placed in a body bag in San Carlos a few weeks before.

Being the driver and the oldest (aged 20), Mark said, 'I'll do all the talking.'

He started to explain the purpose of our quest in his best confident manner, but trailed off a bit when asked to step out of the car and open the boot. Mark was not convinced that one of his passengers did not have a 9mm Pistola Industria Argentina in the boot. I got out too and decided the best tactic was to be almost completely honest, whilst smiling and using all the right body language that I had practised in training on cooperative vehicle checkpoints in Ireland. I showed my ID card and explained that we were just on our way home from the Falklands, and that we had brought back some souvenirs with us that looked like we might also have some guns, but we didn't. She seemed taken aback; the armed police in the background listened carefully, while holding their firearms tighter and moving slowly but surely into a half-circle to cover us all. I then opened the boot and we were suddenly surrounded by a group of police firearms officers, who seemed to be debating whether to spreadeagle us on the bonnet or listen to some war stories?

The stand-off lasted seconds.

The WPC came to my rescue, asking, 'Is that real blood on that helmet?'

'Yes,' I replied. 'Mark took it off a dead Argie.'

This did the trick. A bit of blood and gore grabbed their attention, and they lowered their guard. The smiling young men inside the car making frantic 'thumbs up' signs now just did not seem to be a threat.

Judging by their stout figures and grey hair, some of the armed police were not the team that ran after armed criminals. Maybe they had trained for years and never had the chance to shoot anybody, but no doubt lived in hope. Here in front of them were those young men they had seen yomping across the Falklands for the last few months, who had just come back from a highly successful military campaign and given the Argies a good drubbing. They also had a boot full of potential gisits. Royal Marine Commandos with items taken from the dead enemy! We made quite a stir, and a number of the now very friendly 'Old Bill' crowded around us. They did carry out a search of our bags, but fortunately, we genuinely had no guns. They were so supportive and friendly that we had trouble getting away.

'Guvnor, come and have a look here,' one of them said. 'Royal Marines from the Falklands.' The inspector came over and peered into the boot.

'Bloody hell, are you guys off to war?'

'No, we've just been,' one of the lads answered helpfully.

We chatted with them for a while until one of their number nodded at the queue of cars waiting and said, 'Bloody hell, anyone watching in the queue must think we have stopped the terrorists' car!'

I think we were the same age as some of their kids. They all smiled and wanted to shake our hands, especially when I gave the inspector an Argie helmet belonging to one of the other lads in the car, who momentarily looked a bit miffed but realized it was a small sacrifice to make.

The WPC asked to swap it for the helmet with the blood still inside.

'I will mount that up on the wall of the police bar, he announced, and I could see he was dying to try it on, but members of the public were observing from the queue of cars that were still being held up, so he resisted the temptation. Eventually, off we drove, waving farewell while all the police check team wished us a good leave in return.

BILL'S HOLIDAY

When we came back from the Falklands, the commanding officer, Lieutenant Colonel Vaux, had given us eight weeks' leave – a combination of Easter leave, Summer leave and his generosity. This was great news! I had loads of money in the bank account, as there had not been much use for a chequebook in the South Atlantic, and leave longer than a school summer holiday (which some of us had been on less than two years previously!).

Bill came up with the idea that a group of us could all go to a Spanish holiday resort for a week, just chill out and enjoy the sunny beaches and bars while hanging out with some like-minded girls. As attractive as this idea was, I was in serious need of going home, seeing my family and receiving a bit of home cooking and home comforts. However, we said we would phone each week and try to organize something as leave went on.

As Mark and I were nearing the outskirts of our hometown, having dropped off the other two in Essex, we decided to go straight to our local pub for a drink. We took the added precaution of donning our 'I was in the Falklands' T-shirts, just in case nobody had been watching the news. The PR sergeant, Sergeant 'Del Boy' Martin, had got hold of these T-shirts the day we went on leave; they depicted a marine and a Para kicking an Argentinian soldier off the Falklands. No doubt Sergeant Martin had made another nice tidy profit for his holiday fund too.

The welcome was initially one of caution and interest. It began with some of the locals quietly questioning Mark, who confirmed that 'Yes, we had been "Down South".' We had both grown up on the estate, and between us we knew just about everyone there. News rapidly spread around the pub, and people whom I hadn't really spoken to before started buying us drinks and calling me by my first name. People who I vaguely remembered from school, who had graduated to a 'pub and fags life' and hadn't left the housing estate since leaving school, were suddenly experts on the Falklands conflict and chose to voice their opinion. It was also great to see real friends and neighbours, who had seen us grow up over the years, genuinely wishing us well. All were overly supportive and keen to let us know that they had a relation called Alan Williams who was on HMS *Invincible*, asking whether we knew him. Well, of course a chap can't turn down the opportunity to say, 'What you mean, Bungy Williams.'

'Yeah, that's him, you know him then?' The reply being, 'Nope, never heard of him!'

They always fall for it and look a bit downhearted when you take the piss out of their optimism. Some even asked, 'Did you kill anyone?', which felt a little crass. I had heard of a submariner who had been asked this once in his local pub and replied. 'Well, when we surfaced after sinking the *Belgrano*, we did think it a bit out of order to machine gun the Argies in the water, but that's war.'

Looking back, our mood and feelings were a bit arrogant, but I think that most of it went right over their heads. Judging by the amount of beer they bought us, I don't think we pissed anyone off too much.

Other advantages of being the centre of attention came to light when a very pretty girl handed me a pint and hugged me. 'Welcome home,' she said.

After overtly flirting with her for a while and ignoring the group gathered around Mark, I made a mental note to phone her whilst on leave. I was then dragged into another conversation at the bar, as we seemed to have become minor celebrates with everyone wanting to talk to us. I loved the extra female attention, but some of the blokes got on my nerves by asking daft questions. Maybe it was a mistake wearing the 'I was in the Falklands' T-shirts. I think we'd had enough after a couple of pints and escaped via a side door to head off home at last. The biggest mistake I made on that whole leave, though, was forgetting to get the phone number of the lovely girl. However, I did fortuitously bump into her again a few years later, and am still married to her now!

Leave at home was fantastic! I made the most of home comforts; hot water, clean sheets and Mum's cooking. It was just what was required to put me back into the real world after all that had happened. As I have said, I'd saved quite a bit in the bank as I had not had much to spend it on over the last seven months. Quite frankly, I went a bit over the top with going on the piss and trying my best to sleep with any girl who was interested. But my normally limited success meant that the list didn't get too long. Once I had visited all my friends and drunk too much over too many dinner times, I realized that the world had carried on in the last seven months and it was going to continue, with people worrying about small things too much, For some reason, that annoyed me. I was still fascinated with the luxury of hot running water and dry clothes, yet people were complaining about parking outside of their homes or the latest two-speed hedge cutter that they had just bought but was not working. It was not their fault, but people complaining about what someone had said about someone else's boyfriend, or the local newspaper reporting on a new traffic junction, just did not matter to me!

This couldn't carry on forever, and fortunately, Bill gave me a phone call. He was still keen on the Spanish holiday idea, but we settled for a UK trip around various mates' houses instead – Newcastle, Liverpool, Ipswich and Jersey. We started with Jersey. Jersey was OK, but not all that eventful. However, on the return trip we decided to stop overnight at Weymouth.

We parked my newly purchased Ford Capri in the railway station car park and went off into town. Well, Weymouth turned out to be a far better run ashore than Jersey. We quickly met up with these two girls, who were a right laugh. They seemed to have the same sense of humour as us. Maybe it was because we were in naval territory and were seen as another couple of matelots. However, we thoroughly enjoyed their company, getting pissed, going to a club and talking about outrageous subjects. The girl I had met, Heidi, had a flat, so I was quids in. The girl Bill met, Debbie, lived at home and had slightly old-fashioned parents, so he definitely was not quids in!

Bill came up with the idea that he would go back to the car; he had my spare key, so we separated, and Heidi and I headed back to her flat. Whilst on the way, we walked along the shingle beach, which crunched under our feet, and for the first time since I met her we stopped talking, almost in anticipation of what might or might not happen next.

She stopped and turned towards me, kissed me and just lay down on the beach. Wow! It was fantastic. I was a 19-year-old boy with an obviously experienced 22-year-old young woman, and was taught a great deal, both on the beach and back at her flat.

At about two in the morning, I became aware of a knocking noise. In my bleary, drunken, sex-induced sleep, I was aware that Heidi was calling out of the window. Below in the street was Bill with his friend, Debbie.

'Lew, I've lost my wallet and the cars keys on the beach; can we come in?'

Heidi decided that since we were awake, they may cramp our style, so she refused and we came up with another idea. I threw my car keys out of the window and heartlessly told Bill to crash out in the car. Heidi then carried on with the 'lessons' for the rest of the night. In the morning I even got a bacon sandwich, before Heidi said that she had to go to work, hairdressing for old ladies at a local boutique. I took a slow bimble back to the car, grinning, with that grand feeling of just having had a bag-off. Upon arrival, Bill was asleep in the back of the car, snoring and farting. I got two cups of tea from the nearby railway station and woke him up.

A run ashore debrief followed, with us both feeling on top of the world, laughing about our antics on the beach within about 100 yards of each other, taking time to give a joint appreciative wave from time to time. Bill told me that he had not only lost the spare car key, but also his wallet. He then set of purposefully for the beach to look for his wallet and the key. I was too tired to help and crashed out in the front seat. Bill returned a short while later, chuffed to bits. The tide had been in and out, but he had found both the key and his wallet still intact. As we again spoke of the previous night's events, Bill told me that he had got back to the car and had intended to fold down the back seats and give Debbie 'another one' in the back of the car. When he found out that he had lost the key, they did it on the bonnet. Lo and behold, there on the bonnet was an arse print, with Bill's hands either side. Fantastic, I thought, and I didn't wash the car for months until I had shown brother Steve at home, who found it hilarious, and all the lads at Bickleigh Barracks, who took a detour past my car on the way to the NAFFI to review the forensic evidence still outlined on the now grubby bonnet.

Just at this time, a chap who was on duty in the signal box next to the car park opened the window and shouted, 'Good night was it, lads?', giving us the 'thumbs up', with a big grin on his face.

Bill then realised that he was the signal box nightwatchman and had obviously seen him shagging Debbie on the bonnet of the car in the fully floodlit car park. Another good run ashore!

PHOTO FINISH

ust before Bill left the Corps, we paid another visit to Heidi and Debbie. The lads accused us both of going severely welfare, and joint weddings were mentioned as we refused yet another weekend in Guz (Plymouth) on the piss with the usual crowd. We grabbed a bag full of our best dancing gear and headed off for the known and certain delights of Weymouth. We received severe flak shouted at us from the windows of our grots until we shut the door of my trusty Capri (bonnet still unwashed but fading) and roared off up Bickleigh Lane.

We met up at Heidi's flat, and after some initial knowing smirks were exchanged, we got over our sober and slightly embarrassed reunion. They had arranged a fairly normal night out at a local club with some of their friends, and we met up with a large group of them in a pub first. Bill, as usual, charmed them with his wacky, risqué jokes. Some introduced themselves with sly smiles and said, 'Are you the two marines who took Heidi and Debbie to the beach?'

The group giggled and gave us knowing glances, having no doubt heard all the gory details. We were outnumbered three-to-one, so we just sat back modestly and smiled, knowing full well that we were getting the piss taken out of us; but hey, we didn't care! Heidi and Debbie must have told them all what a giggle they'd had that night on the beach, and I don't think Bill and I faired too badly in the performance stakes. We enjoyed the attention of this group of girls taking the piss out of us, in fact we lapped it up. Bill jokingly boasted of his larger-than-average 'piss hard', which is one of those erections that you get at a certain stage of inebriation that just won't go away, even if you bash it on the edge of a kitchen table (so Bill tells me).

The night progressed nicely, with Bill and I being far too generous on the rounds of drink, but most of the girls tried to buy us one in return.

By this time of the year, it was getting far too cold for beach activities, so the four of us went back to Heidi's flat and all sat on the settee, chatting and drinking.

Bill started trying to get off with Debbie, and Heidi made a suggestion that we should leave them alone and go to the bedroom. Bill then came up with an idea that he had no doubt hatched some weeks before. He explained his imminent departure from the Corps and that he wanted something to impress his mates before he left. He produced a green beret and a camera from his bag and asked the girls if they were up for it.

Debbie was, but Heidi took some persuading. However, it all turned out OK in the end.

On the Monday before Bill left the Corps, he proudly pinned this photo on the company noticeboard next to the company commander's Daily Orders. There was Bill, wearing nothing other than his green beret and a stupid grin. He was lying on his back, smartly saluting at the camera, whilst Debbie and Heidi posed on either side of him holding onto his erect 8in chosp!

BURIAL AT SEA

hilst at Royal Marines Poole, in Dorset, it was quite a common request for ex-Royal Marines who had passed away to have their ashes scattered in Poole Harbour, the home of the RM Landing Craft Branch. Heroic chaps who had landed on the Normandy beaches on D-Day considered that it was a small and achievable request, and had this clause written into their wills. This was in the 1980s, and many Second World War veterans were passing away at the time. If every request had been honoured in full, the Royal Marines Landing Craft Branch would have spent all their time as a maritime funeral service, but they always did their best.

There was also the problem of the deceased marine's elderly relatives with walking sticks or in wheelchairs, who were not all that keen about boarding a flat-bottomed landing craft in winter and heading out into the stormy English Channel, just to honour the memory of Uncle Albert – who had bored them all their lives with stories of opposed landings on enemy shores. They didn't want to get first-hand experience of a rolling landing craft at sea or have a few cheeky waves slap off the front of the ramp and cover their best funeral suits and dresses with cold, wet saltwater.

A compromise was reached, and the ex-servicemen's last requests were invariably carried out at the end of the landing craft pier. This meant that elderly relatives could dodder or be wheeled out along the pier with the unit padre, and after a short service in the blustery, onshore wind, they could seek the comfort of their warm cars again and carry on to the wake, to toast their fallen comrade or loved family member.

However, the business of the day had to carry on, and often maintenance was being carried out on the moored landing craft warped onto the pier as a funeral service was held at the end of the wooden structure. Landing craft rates[14] might be painting the tank deck while engineers carried out checks on the winch equipment and engines.

Following a solemn and poignant speech, the padre would scatter the ashes from the urn by tipping them into Poole Harbour on the outgoing tide. Occasionally, this would coincide with an onshore wind, and the ashes would be gathered up by an unpredicted gust and whisked along and under the wooden pier, swirling around the various moored landing craft which were there. The ashes would be carried up and over the gunwale and into the tank deck area, where they would settle on the fresh grey paint being daubed on by the unfortunate marine detailed off for this task that day.

As the funeral party were wheeled back slowly along the pier by their equally elderly companions, often supported by walking sticks, they may have noticed the occasional marine in green overalls dripping and chuntering as he emptied the dustpan and brush containing a grey earthy substance into the nearest skip, with a look of being more than slightly annoyed, thinking that last gust had picked up some grey sand from the nearby beach and ruined his paintwork.

The padre would take this opportunity to mention how lucky the party were to have had such good weather for the service that day, and was that a Ringed Plover flying past on the other side of the pier? He did his best to increase the pace from a crawling dodder to a slow shuffle so that the party would get off the pier and avoid any awkward questions.

Upon reflection, I suppose the deceased veteran might quite like the idea of being partially incorporated into the paint of the tank deck on a modern-day Royal Marines landing craft, to travel around the world and carry out a few beach landings on foreign shores again.

---

14. Rate is a naval qualification; in this case, someone qualified to work on landing craft.

DEFENCE MINISTER INVITED IN FOR TEA

Once in a while, an important politician would visit the unit whilst on exercise. They must use the same script as visiting major generals, as all their questions were basically the same: 'How long have you been in the Corps/Branch?' 'What do you think of this exercise/the dreadful local customs/the poor?' Etc., etc.

Politicians had the additional responsibility of asking bone[15] questions about equipment. If it was, for example, the Defence Minister – and therefore in charge of UK and NATO strategic decisions – they obviously didn't need to know or have a clue about how or why the most basic piece of military hardware worked and what its capabilities were. This fact was cause for some concern when demonstrating and assisting visiting politicians on rifle ranges. Weapons instructors could be heard politely pointing out, 'No, Sir, the bullets come out of that end.' And, 'Yes Sir, it does make a loud bang, that would be the bullets coming out of the hole.'

Here was the person in charge of our Trident nuclear submarines, with enough power to devastate most of Russia on the authority of a phone call, and he closed his eyes when firing a rifle because the bangs were too loud.

Most of the NCOs were polite to such visitors, the most rebellious they got being to make 'Sir' sound like an insult. Some of the marines

---

15. Bone question: From 'throw someone a bone', or a really easy, obvious question, when it's more about being seen asking a question than genuinely wanting to know what someone thinks.

couldn't resist it when asked about new equipment that they were using, and they knew the risks they were taking when a visiting minister pointed to a part of the weapon and asked a bone question. 'That's the phaser attachment, Sir.' (Modern weapons do actually have these, but they didn't then.)

'Marvellous, just like *Star Wars*,' would be the reply from the minister, no doubt not wishing to look silly. Then he would frown, thinking, 'That's a bit James Bond-like, I didn't know we had those yet', before quickly moving on.

On this one particular occasion, we were in Norway and the Company Quarter Master Sergeant (CQMS) detailed our ten-man tent off to cook an Arctic ration pack for the visiting Defence Minister, Michael Heseltine, with instructions to ensure that he got a cup of tea. The CO would also be attending, so we had to look after him as well.

Arctic ration packs are dehydrated rations, but they also have loads of nutty chocolate in them. They contain up to 5,000 calories per day, most of which are consumed by hungry active marines, yomping along on skis carrying huge Bergens. Melted snow is used to rehydrate the ration pack, and is in great abundance in Norway in the winter. This saved carrying water, which is very heavy in the quantities needed to keep you healthy and fit in the Arctic.

The CQMS issued us with a large teapot from stores in order to make a decent brew of tea rather than melting snow in a mess tin. 'Bungy' Williams filled this pot with fresh snow and started to melt it, adding more as required. Word came around that the visiting party was running late and that they would only have time for a cup of tea. The CO was keen to show the minister how comfortable the living conditions could be at minus 30°C in a tent. In due course, the CO and Mr Heseltine came into our tent and sat down on packs. They were given chocolate and waited expectantly for their tea. Bungy duly served up the tea in new black pint (pussers') mugs, also issued by the CQMS. The normal conversation ensued, although to be fair, the minister did seem to know what he was on about. But you just can't help thinking that ministers always seem to be delighted to meet the 'poor' (us marines, in this case), and are especially pleased when they don't throw abuse or flour and eggs at them. So, by the light of a Coleman gas lamp, the tea was drunk, and after shaking hands and thanking us, the Defence Minister and CO left.

Shortly afterwards, the CQMS arrived. 'Bungy, don't think you are going to prof my teapot and mugs. Hand them over.'

Bungy went outside of the tent to empty the teapot. We then heard the CQMS and Bungy cracking up laughing. Upon exploring the source of the joke, they were both looking into the teapot, and at the bottom, swirling around, were small clusters of reindeer shit, just like rabbit droppings. Bungy must have scooped it up when collecting snow for the brew. Fantastic – we had just served the Defence Minister and CO reindeer shit tea, and he had thanked us. Much more subtle than throwing eggs and flour!

ARCTIC ANTICS

odily functions are always a problem in the great outdoors. Add three layers of clothing, on a snowy windswept plateau at minus 30ºC, plus three days on compo rations, and the bowels will refuse to follow orders.

Compo rations are a compact method of feeding troops high-calorie, high-quality food, and they come in various daily menus. Go on a ten-day exercise and you will eat the same menu at least twice, then for the rest of your military career, the novelty has worn off. Bearing in mind some serve twenty-two years or longer, that makes a lot of servings of dehydrated chicken supreme.

The temperate climate ration packs contain 3,000 calories, enough to keep you marching or digging in for twenty-four hours. The dehydrated Arctic rations, as I have said, have 5,000 calories, enough to keep you yomping along on skis with a 90lb pack and rifle for twenty-four hours. In the Arctic, the body uses masses of calories just to stay warm, let alone the demands that fighting in such conditions puts on the energy reserves. The Arctic ration also consists of two bars of chocolate and two packets of Rolos. Again, a fantastic discovery when you first open one, but any marine or ex-marine who buys Rolos must be a masochist!

Decision time regarding bodily functions comes after about twenty-four hours. Do I keep regular, and bare my arse to the full wrath of nature? Or do I:

a. Hope that the exercise finishes early, despite the briefing and multi-million pounds spent on the planning stage?

b. Depend on some local, whom I might or might not meet, having a head (toilet) in a nice warm and dry house that they would let me, and all my mates, use?

c. Get casevaced (an emergency casualty evacuation) after an injury, hopefully not too scary an injury, which could by its very nature negate the necessity of finding a head anyway?

d. Hang on for the whole ten-day exercise as we are catching an RAF plane home straight afterwards, and it's always such fun to leave your 'excess baggage' with the RAF?

After one such exercise, we were taken to an airfield in northern Norway to await the RAF in some VC10s. (Note: the RAF are affectionately known as 'crabs', because whenever volunteers are asked for, they are supposed to step sideways until they are out of view of anyone who may detail them off.)

We were to put up some ten-man tents as a temporary shelter on the edge of the airfield, get fed, have duty frees issued and collect our kit; a well-organized plan which for once worked. The only problem was that 'Crab Air' couldn't make it. The weather conditions had caused a whiteout, which is when you literally can't see more than a foot in front of you because of the wind whipping up loose snow and causing dangerous drifts.

Bugger! This meant that we would have to spend another night in Norway under canvas and catch our flights the next day. So we got out our smelly sleeping bags once more. Since we were non-tactical, we didn't need to have any watch system, which meant we could all get a good night's sleep. The bowels would have to wait.

'Me shit-lockers toppers, Sergeant Major,' was the conclusion of many unhappy campers.

Well, it was very nice and organized for them to issue us with our duty-frees before we flew, and it seemed a shame to have an early night. So out came the cards and the pint pussers' mugs from our water bottles. Amongst the eight of us, we had a selection of spirits that would do justice to any line of optics in a well-supplied pub, but no mixers. Melted snow wasn't an option, because who knows what sort of *crap* you would find in that on an airfield. We also didn't have any money to gamble with. Someone suggested Rolos, but they were quickly slagged off. So we ended up playing a game called 'Chase the pisser', with the forfeit for losing being to drink a finger's width of your chosen poison.

As the game progressed, the neat spirit quickly had the desired effect, with some quite quickly turning into burbling heaps. This no doubt built up Taff's courage. 'It's no good, I am going outside. I may be some time,' he said, resigned to the inevitable.

With this, he followed in the footsteps of previous famous, intrepid British Antarctic explorers of Captain Scott's party, and disappeared into the freezing swirling night. However, unlike Captain Oates, he returned a short while later, with his prize proudly mounted on a snow shovel! It was a huge, a Mr Whippy, even with a tapered curly end. The freezing conditions had frozen the turd almost solid within a few minutes.

'Ugh, get it out of here,' came the amused but worried cries.

Taff was pissed and could have at any moment dropped the prize on some poor bastard's sleeping bag. (First rule of the Arctic – it's bad for morale having a large turd poised on your green slug for the night.)

Taff disappeared outside again and returned, chortling to himself, minus the snow shovel and contents.

The card school carried on. The neat Bacardi that I was drinking was also having the desired effect. Fortunately, I was one of those who remained regular on exercise, so I didn't have the same problems as some of my oppos. However, as the night progressed, I started to have difficulty focusing on my cards; others had difficulty focusing on retaining their extra baggage as the alcohol was having a laxative effect.

Nick then decided that enough was enough, and out he went. So as not to be outdone, he too returned with his even larger frozen solid Mr Whippy on the snow shovel, and with a whirling of spin drift someone quickly heaved him outside. He returned giggling at his original highly amusing performance. Burt made his objections known in his whiny Birmingham accent: 'That's disgusting, yow fooking animals. This isn't a, "see who can do the biggest Mr Whippy" competition.'

There's something about a Brum accent that makes you want to disagree with whatever they are dripping about, even if they've got a good point.

Tiny decided to have a go next. 'When you've got to go, you've got to go,' he said, opening the tent flaps in a resigned manner and striding into the whiteout.

The game continued for a short while.

'Tiny's taking his time,' someone mentioned. The rest of us had reached the stage where we didn't really care.

'Open the door,' Tiny was heard to shout from outside. 'I need a hand.' Burt opened the door and Tiny's large frame fought its way into the tent past the door flaps. Tiny looked mighty pleased with himself. Red-faced, with a broad grin and holding out in front of him the snow shovel containing the most enormous turd you have ever seen. It was like a curled-up python and filled the best part of the shovel. We all burst out laughing, except Burt. It looked as if Tiny had won the competition with his outstanding contribution, assisted by ten days on compo. Just then, Nick leapt up and inspected the monster at close range.

'Cheating bastard! Look,' protested Nick.

On closer inspection, we could clearly see thumbprints where Tiny had obviously joined the previous two turds together and added his own contribution. He was unanimously disqualified, between roars of laughter that must have echoed all around the tented encampment.

LOM BAR

We were once accommodated at a picturesque town in southern Norway called Lom. This place hadn't experienced the cutting edge of NATO's Northern Flank before, so when 600 Royal Marines turned up and the Ministry of Defence paid good money to use their otherwise-unused summer hotels and mountain accommodation, they no doubt thought they were quids in. Someone once described Norwegians as a race of 3 million alcoholics clinging to some cold rocks; a very unfair and inaccurate statement. The last census counted the population to be at least 3.5 million.

I couldn't see how they could afford to drink. Whiskey at the time was £40 a bottle, while in the UK it was just £5. A pint of beer was £2.50, when in the UK it was only £1 a pint. The Norwegian government set the tax on alcohol at a colossal rate in an effort to prevent alcohol abuse. Our UK government has since set similar tax rates, and it seems to work here just as well as it worked in Norway in the 1980s – everyone still gets 'Harry Crappers' on Friday and Saturday night and starts fights, but they are poor on Monday.

We had a far more lucrative trick up our sleeves.

A useful bunch of people to take with you to Norway is the NAAFI stores, as they bring with them duty-free beer, tobacco and spirits. Add to this a hotel bar and several hundred marines, plus a naïve local population desperate for cheap booze, and you instantly get the most popular venue in southern Norway. That may not be saying much, but we didn't even have to try. Clubs nowadays would spend thousands of pounds on promoting such a successful venue as emerged at Lom Bar.

Initially, the locals treated us with mild suspicion, as some wag had sent the story around that we were a penal battalion (for whom it was prison or join the marines). I expect it was someone in one of the fighting Companies who had been sent to one of the scenic but unpopulated mountain hotels, with several lakes and space to ski but very few bars and women. At the weekends, it was amazing how many ration runs and store runs had to be carried out from these outlying locations. What was equally amazing was that so many marines volunteered to give their weekends up to help the CQMS hump the stores around.

Some of the lads worked with the local caretakers and hotel workers, and these people were slowly invited into our bar. All were bought many drinks and a good night was had by everyone. Lars, the caretaker, questioned the prices we were charging and his eyes went the size of saucers when I confirmed that the list was correct. Most Norwegians speak very good English as a second language, which puts us all to shame. The American influence and the film industry no doubt helped. Lars taught me how to say, 'Have you any older sisters?' in Norwegian, and other equally useful phrases.

The UK influence was no doubt from football and the music scene of the 1980s new wave. We had a good PR sergeant, who kept the record collection updated and set up the disco in the bar. The only Norwegian band to have made it on the international scene was A-Ha, so anything by the Beatles through to punk rock got everyone dancing.

'Come again with some friends,' we said to Lars and his pals as they staggered out of the bar, clutching the remains of £20 worth of whiskey in an open bottle of scotch under his coat. The next night, word had obviously got around and the bar was heaving. The blokes got drunk – encouraged by the prices and the generosity of the lads, especially if they had girlfriends with big tits – and the girls thought we were different and very funny.

As a bloke, it's a bastard when some new smoothie turns up and the girls in your group say, 'Oh, he's so different and not like all the rest', and he promptly shags the girl you've been doing the groundwork on for weeks. Well, it was now my turn to be different. It was a win-win situation. I think some of the local blokes got pissed off, but I found the Norwegians of Lom and the surrounding communities very open in their outlook, particularly when their boyfriends were left drunk on a table in the bar on duty-free whiskey, whilst the girls were shown what the hotel accommodation looked like in winter.

The Beatles were always a popular request made by locals, and the DJ usually obliged, whilst no doubt hoping to convert them all to The Stranglers and The Jam by the end of the tour. Meanwhile, in my hotel room, I was hoping that the Norwegian wood construction of my bed was as reliable as the timber that Paul McCartney was singing about in the bar.

TAFF SERVES UP SUPPER

Meanwhile, the officers were having a far duller time. The more senior officers were used to entertaining local dignitaries in the mess, all dressed up in mess dress, and very smart they looked too. These mess nights usually took place to commemorate the Battle of Trafalgar or some other Corps memorable date. Most senior officers were dead keen on these nights, as it gave them a chance to spin their own stories to a captive audience about Aden, Malaya and Northern Ireland when it was really bad in the early days of the conflict. The poor YOs (Young Officers) were not so keen on these events; they were, after all, young blokes as well and had joined for excitement in foreign climes, yet here they were escorting elderly Norwegian couples into the mess for a very civilized high-class dinner with all the trimmings and a gentle evening of entertainment. Sometimes there was even a string quartet in the corner of the room. Even worse, the senior officers might start spinning stories of their time as YOs in Aden and other far-flung places.

Meanwhile, the daughters and granddaughters of the local dignitaries were busy in the bar directly underneath the officers' mess, getting drunk and leaping around the dance floor to Duran Duran and Spandau Ballet, with young marines ogling them and hoping to trap off.

There were places in the world where the officers' mess and the standard of food and entertainment they received would be envied by the non-commissioned ranks. Lom was not one of those places.

A couple of young officers got in the shit one night for gate-crashing the bar in full mess dress after one such formal do. Before visiting the commanding officer the following morning, they were seen absolutely 'shitters', leaping around the dance floor and trying to trap off with some bemused local girl who couldn't understand why these otherwise good-looking young chaps insisted on dressing up like penguins.

I am sure that the officers didn't do too badly, as they did have the full backup of better accommodation, chefs who could be cajoled into providing food for private parties, and mess NCOs who were experts at acquiring alcohol at short notice in the wee hours of the morning.

One evening, the commanding officer, along with several other officers, were having a private party in the CO's and major's lodge. Just the two of them were accommodated in this very fine log cabin for the three-month tour. Invited along were a handful of influential councillors and their partners, and no doubt some women who'd already had their husbands nobbled by the cheap whiskey that the mess NCO had provided earlier on in the evening during the excellent mess dinner produced by Taff, the officers' mess chef, and his team of catering staff. The CO had got Taff to sort out some nibbles and lay them out on his dining table in the lodge, awaiting the arrival of the small party. The CO was keen to impress the inebriated party of VIPs and show off his accommodation and the picturesque view across the valley to Lom church and the frozen lake in the background, all highlighted by a fresh fall of snow.

He enthusiastically drew the curtains back from the picture window, whilst extolling the virtues of this wonderful country to the collection of nodding, politely smiling, convinced individuals. When the curtains were whisked back, there was the view down the valley as expected, but no gasps of appreciation came from the stunned and now silent group. What wasn't expected was the view into the nearby hotel room, where Taff, the chef, had his curtains wide open.

'Oh my gawd!' the major exclaimed as the whole party stood there, jaws dropping open in stunned silence.

Taff was going at it hammer and tongs, doing it doggy-style with Ingrid, one of the blonde kitchen helpers and daughter to one of the local councillors, now in the CO's log cabin. Her hands were gripping the bed head whilst she bent forward, and judging by her face, was obviously enjoying the jolly old thing. Taff, with his full chef's uniform still on, but his blue-and-white checked chef's trousers down around his knees, served up the main course. His chef's apron, tied at his waist, was neatly draped over the naked girl's back.

DRUGS BUST

Every once in a while, a weekend had to be spent on duty in the guardroom. This included main-gate sentry and wandering patrol. Even though the terrorist threat was high from the IRA, we still used to patrol with just large pickaxe handles. I think the visual presence was sufficient. Seeing two Royal Marines patrolling the camp boundaries, anyone who knew how we operated in Ireland would be aware of the professionalism of the Corps, and this was a deterrent on its own.

I think that Whitehall and the Home Office at that time were not that keen on letting trained professional soldiers carry live ammo on mainland UK. Better to leave that for Northern Ireland and other places around the world. The British public would surely be alarmed if British soldiers were seen actually carrying armed guns on the mainland!

How things have moved on. When the Twin Towers in New York were hit, we had tanks outside Heathrow Airport and dubious authority given to shoot suicide bomb suspects in the head in central London. It has now become normal to see armed police in public.

In 1989, the real negligence was revealed when the same risk-averse and money-saving thinking by political planners put unarmed civilian guards on the gates of mainland military camps, leaving an open invitation for the bombing of Deal Barracks.

However, prior to this attack, I had reached the dizzying heights of corporal and was on duty as guard commander at Deal when a group of SIB investigators and MPs turned up at the gate. They called me into the back room of the guardroom and informed me that they had a report that a Royal Marine had been using drugs and they were going to search his room. I was required to lead them to the room. Out came a black

Labrador from the back of a van, all ready to start his sniffer dog duties, and off we headed to the poor unfortunate's room.

Once found, I felt it was my duty to explain to the marine why they were there. I was quickly told to stand back and not meddle in such matters that I did not understand; this was, after all, a highly trained service drugs squad and I was a mere guard commander corporal.

When we entered the room, the three marines in the shared billet looked a tad surprised. The suspect was identified and told to open his locker. The sergeant in charge obviously enjoyed informing his victims that his team was very important, and he wasn't going to have some jumped-up corporal stealing all his best lines. (He had spent a long time rehearsing them in front of a mirror, I expect.) He also mentioned how the search would be carried out and said that if anything was damaged or destroyed during a negative search, there may be financial compensation.

The suspect stood to one side and the sniffer dog was let go.

'Go on boy, seek it out,' the handler instructed. The black Labrador went for it full out, tail wagging and bashing off everyone's legs and against the open locker door. The dog went like a black torpedo straight for a zip-up pusser's holdall.

'Is it in there, boy?' the handler encouraged him, unzipping the bag.

The sergeant said, 'OK lad if that's where your stash is, you might as well cough to it now.'

'It's only my washing. I've just come back from a dobie run [a trip to the launderette],' the marine said in his defence.

The dog pushed his head into the bag, and the bag was moved around the bottom of the locker with some force as the dog tried to get his teeth into the suspect package at the very bottom.

Out came the dog's triumphant head, tail still wagging, with a large round brown shape with clear plastic wrapping in his mouth.

Just before the dog had time to wolf down the large pork pie, the word 'Ginsters' could be read as part of the crust fell onto the floor before the dog eagerly bolted that down too, wrapper and all.

'OK, I'll pay you for the pork pie now,' the red-faced dog handler said, and dipped his hand into his own pocket and paid the marine a 50 pence piece. The sergeant was equally as livid that his team had been made to look foolish because no drugs had been found, as he was that the dog handler had shown weakness, apologized and paid for the pork pie. The instructions were that 'MAYBE' financial compensation would be paid.

The 'crack' team left. The only one without their tail between their legs was the black Labrador, whose tail continued to wag all the way back to the guardroom. He'd had a smashing walk and met some new friends who had given him a large Ginsters pork pie.

This sergeant is probably standing at the entrance to a car park in a town centre somewhere today, issuing tickets, having failed to get into the local constabulary after his twenty-two years in the service.

JACKING UP TRANSPORT

At the end of a good run ashore, wherever you are in the world, there always comes the homing beacon phase. This is the point when a bloke realizes that he is not going to get a bag off, has had big eats and now all he wants to do is get his head down, preferably in his own pit; be it at home, on a ship or in a barracks somewhere.

In my experience, the transport home falls into two categories: legal and proffed. Legal would include demands with menaces from some friend who did not particularly want to go the 7 miles to Bickleigh Barracks when they live in Plymouth. It could also include some passing Norwegian 'good Samaritan' on a snowy mountain road at night, who, out of the goodness of his heart, had stopped to see what was wrong. After all, no one in their right mind would be walking along a Norwegian road in minus 30 degrees, so there must have been an accident somewhere. The Samaritan would then be asked politely if he could offer a lift, whilst several drunken smelly Royal Marines got in the back.

The normal meaning of 'proffing' seems to have been lost on most civvy police forces when it comes to transport, because this category includes all bikes, boats, go-karts and pedalos, which were going to be returned the following morning in any case, if only a chap could remember where the transport was proffed from! This second form normally occurs when a bloke is with his mates and gets that urge to 'perform'. If a chap was on his own, he would normally put up with a long, sobering, lonely walk home.

Every Friday morning at 42 Commando, the whole unit would line up for PE on the parade ground, and would then set off in companies and run around the edges of Dartmoor. The RSM was very proud of his fitness and liked to take centre stage on these occasions, using the occasion to put his point of view across concerning some issue that was getting up his or the CO's nose.

Friday morning, being traditionally after Thursday evening, meant that many of the participants were suffering heavily from the effects of a good run ashore in Plymouth the night before. This was not a problem; we were all young, fit and immortal. After the first mile, people would normally feel better, even if they had to chuck up in a passing hedge and then get back in the ranks.

What did cause concern to the RSM one Friday morning was the dumper truck parked in the middle of the parade ground. The barracks had no roadworks going on at that time, but the top of Bickleigh Lane 3 miles away did. The CO was oblivious, but the RSM quickly got the CSMs together and passed the word that the dumper truck had better be delivered back to the roadworks ASAP or someone would dip out severely.

Several giggles could be heard from M Company lines, which stopped as soon as the RSM glared in their direction. This was not proof, but was good enough for the RSM and M Company's cards to be marked.

The dumper truck was spirited back to the top of Bickleigh Lane, but word had already gotten around that several Booties had been yomping back to Bickers on the dark evening before when one had the idea of starting the dumper truck. The others got into the bucket, and they all chugged down Bickleigh Lane, saluting the main gate sentry as he opened the barrier for them. They then parked it on the parade ground, forgetting that it was PE day the following morning.

The RSM went ballistic when a JCB was on the parade ground first thing one subsequent Friday morning as all ranks lined out for PE. K Company, so as not to be outdone, had decided to use this as their staff car that evening. There were even kebab wrappers in the bucket that the occupants had been munching on during the trip back. Phone calls were made, and again a driver delivered the JCB back to the roadworks. Warnings were given out verbally on the parade ground, and more officially with less colourful language on Daily Orders promulgated on every noticeboard around camp. That would no doubt do the trick, the RSM thought.

The following week, I was with a few mates in Plymouth on a Thursday night, having had a skin full, and the homing beacons had been set off. Yet again, we had all almost trapped off with some 'essence pash', but not quite. Maybe the next time we saw them, they would whisk us off to Plymouth Hoe or some other romantic location, where they would no doubt give us a good seeing too. We were just unlucky tonight! Various comments could be heard, such as 'I thinned her out just to play hard to get' or 'I would have gone back to her flat, but I thought I would join you lot for big eats instead'.

We were in the taxi queue, complying with the RSM's instructions, when all of a sudden, a double-decker bus pulled up next to us. This was not an out-of-the-ordinary event in one of the main streets in Plymouth, but seeing Jim behind the wheel certainly was. He had only left us five minutes before for a Kentucky Fried Chicken and said he would catch us up. No doubt Jim had decided to perform and play to a crowd, but also 'black cat' (i.e., outdo) the previous Friday morning's PE sessions.

The doors opened up. 'All aboard, inexact fares only, first stop Bickleigh Barracks,' shouted a grinning Jim from the driver's seat. I honestly gave it two seconds thought as to how wise this action was, but quickly realized that soon all the seats would be taken, so I boarded as instructed. Off we went, the bus making further stops as 'oppos' were recognized along the route and additional passengers were picked up. We even picked up a couple of girls on their way to Mutley Plane, which was on the way back to barracks anyway. Some of the lads tried a last-ditch effort to trap off with them, inviting them to deliver the bus back to Plymouth once the jolly old thing had been done at Bickers. The girls politely refused with a giggle and got off at the next stop.

The bus travelled on, straight past the Area HQ of the local police force and onto Bickleigh Lane. By this time Cliff Richard's 'We're All Going on a Summer Holiday' had broken out and was being sung at full voice all the way down Bickleigh Lane, we having gained full confidence in Jim's PSV driving ability. We also knew that if we were stopped at this point, we could all outrun some fat country copper and be in our beds before reinforcements arrived.

Again, we passed the main gate sentry, who only kept the barrier down long enough to recognize Jim, then raised it with a chortle and a request to the guard commander shortly afterwards, who was too busy watching telly, to be relieved from the gate, just to confuse the timings of any follow-up enquiry.

The following morning, Jim woke up and bimbled to the heads, with a towel wrapped around him, in a drunken haze. He looked out of the window overlooking the parade ground and said, 'What the fu...?' as the whole sorry tale came back to him.

We all fell in as normal, but this time the local civvy police were already all over the bus with fingerprint experts and photographers.

The RSM never found out who had proffed the bus, but the whole guard from Thursday evening found themselves on watch non-stop for the rest of the weekend.

CLOSE SCRAPES

In any group of young men, there are always those that will cause trouble. Add alcohol, and the trouble just gets worse. The ever-present danger of getting in the shit with the Corps generally kept most larks under control and just within the law. There were, of course, times when this line was crossed, as with most young men growing up. The knack was to not mix whilst ashore with those who would always get in the shit, but back up your own oppos and then all disappear very fast together when the police arrive.

One night in Plymouth, after a skin full, Steve, Ronnie and I made our way back to our regular taxi office on Union Street. We were such regular customers that Bob, the owner of the firm, looked after us and seemed to appreciate that we never gave his staff a hard time or did runners from his taxis. We would even sit and eat our big eats in the taxi office rather than the back of the car. This agreement meant that we always got a taxi back to Bickleigh at a reasonable price at any time of the night.

This particular night, we were sitting in the taxi office waiting for our ride. I was tackling a KFC, with three pieces of chicken and fries, and had just gotten to the stage of munching the crunchy bits on the end of the bones when I became aware of a disturbance. A local man was giving his girlfriend some stick whilst waiting in the office, shouting at her. That was just about tolerable, but then he started to swear at her and kick her violently in the legs. I had no idea how this had built up, as I had been engrossed with Colonel Sanders. Ronnie walked up to Bob and simply asked in his Glaswegian accent, 'Bob, you want him out of here?'

Bob nodded urgently from behind his glass screen, and with this, Ronnie grabbed hold of the bloke by the back of his collar and heaved him out of the door backwards. The bloke looked startled as he disappeared through the door and was unceremoniously put on his arse outside. He got up, but instead of challenging Ronnie he just ran off. Bob, in the meantime, had organized the next taxi for the young girl who had been abused and kicked. We sat back and felt good about ourselves. Bob thanked us and offered us the next taxi, as long as all in the queue were happy with this. They also agreed, pleased that the drunken thug had been removed quickly without further trouble. I was just about to finish off the dregs of the chicken gravy with an index finger when about seven blokes turned up, led by the young man whom we had last seen disappearing through the door with the help of Ronnie.

This 'hero' identified us to his mates as the three who had just beaten him up, and all started to take stances and jostle with each other, surrounding the exit in a semi-circle. Ronnie immediately went outside, followed by Steve. I just thought, 'Oh well, we are all going to get filled in, but at least we will put up a good fight together.' The thought of doing a runner on your mates just did not occur to any of us.

Steve and I stood just outside the door of the taxi rank, with our backs to the wall and some dustbins, while Ronnie was behind us and was gobbing off at the 'magnificent seven' who were led and egged on by the idiot who had just beaten his girlfriend. We gained confidence as we faced off all seven with just the three of us; maybe they were trying to comprehend the Glaswegian insults that Ronnie was hurling at them, but his body language was easily read. I was amazed that the seven of them just stood there, making gestures and waiting for us to make the first move. None of them seemed to actually want to start a fight.

We had reached a stand-off, which Ronnie decided to see if he could take advantage of. I heard one of the dustbin lids being removed and then Ronnie triumphantly shout, 'Come on then you wankers, if you are going to start a fight let's get on with it!'

I turned slightly and saw that Ronnie had just found the world's biggest magnum bottle of champagne in the bin, and was now brandishing it like a club over his head. Not to be outdone, Steve picked up the dustbin lid and held it like a shield. I just felt that the odds had been evened, and considered that maybe we would not end up in the hospital, but in the police station instead.

Police sirens could be heard, as Bob had been quick to put in a call, only to look outside and be horrified that his good Samaritans were about to be nicked for carrying weapons in the street as a result of his call. Fortunately, the magnificent seven ran off and Steve clanged the bin lid back on the dustbin. I grappled Ronnie back and disarmed him as the police turned the corner, their headlights illuminating the scene.

Bob ushered all three of us into the back of the nearest taxi, jumped into the driver's seat and drove off. The buzz of coming out on top of a situation where we were almost certain to have been filled in but more than saved face was electric. Bob dropped us off and would not accept a fee. For the rest of my time in Plymouth, Bob always remembered us and provided a VIP service at a substantially reduced rate for his Bickleigh Boys.

THE GAMEL DANCE

In southern Norway, the main entertainment on weekends, during the long dark winter nights, is the Gamel Dance. This is in effect a barn dance, with local harpsichord players sitting on the stage whilst the whole community whirls around on the dance floor in an anticlockwise direction, in a 'waltz-meets-the-ho-down' frenzy. This may sound exciting enough, but sometimes a particularly rebellious harpsichord player will get them all going clockwise instead!

People from every part of the community attend these events, bringing with them their prize moonshine. This is a sugar alcohol made in stills inside mountainside dwellings under many a kitchen sink. The local garages even sell rum and whiskey essence in small racks to improve this mind-blowing rocket fuel's flavour (or make it drinkable). As part of the local community, we felt obliged to attend such events and support local traditions.

This was normally planned in the hotel bar in Lom when it became obvious that we were not going to trap that night. The level of obviousness was in direct proportion to the amount of alcohol drunk, but the night was young and our kidneys were immortal. So what if the bar shut at 11.30; we were still up for it and would scrounge a lift from someone in the bar with the promise of a bottle of whiskey the next time we saw them. Off we headed into the hills, not having a clue where we were being taken and normally ending up at a cold and dark windswept village with a central community barn. Upon entering the barn, all was warm, lively and loud, food was sometimes served, but more to the point, many local girls who wouldn't be seen dead in the Lom hotel bar were present in their droves. As always, the local young bucks could be relied upon to get absolutely shitfaced very early on and be seen lying on tables and crashing out in cars outside. Any who were still sober would be dancing around the floor on their own, a bottle of moonshine in one hand whilst spinning to the latest harpsichord sounds. This presented a number of opportunities to us as temporary members of the community. The girls were open and welcoming, especially if you asked them to dance. All those years as a member of the Royal Marines Formation Dance Display Unit in the night clubs of Plymouth were not put to waste.

Another attraction was to steal the drunken Norwegians' moonshine. This was a very easy game, as most of the victims were asleep in a drunken heap at the time. Resistance was only met if some other local had thought he spotted the bottle first. These minor disagreements were soon sorted out amicably without resorting to violence.

One such visit to a Gamel Dance found Tiny, Appy and me mooching around in a crowded swirl of dancers flinging themselves about in a clockwise direction around the barn in a moonshine-enhanced frenzy. On a table nearby were two sleeping Norwegians, lulled forward in a drunken stupor, their heads resting on the crook of their arms. A naval press gang would have thought it their lucky day walking into a Gamel Dance.

In between the unconscious figures was a lonely bottle, which looked three-quarters full. This was a good-enough indicator as to the vintage of this brew, so we promptly proffed it, clearly to prevent any further deterioration of the brain cells of the two previous owners. We passed the bottle around, sampling the aroma, guessing that it was from a westerly facing outhouse 2,000ft up a rocky V-shaped valley, giving off the bouquets of the bleach and sheep dip stored in the dodgy containers underneath the kitchen sink. Actually, it wasn't all that bad. It was smooth, but with an obviously high alcohol content. Whiskey essence must have been used to improve the flavour, and it turned out to be quite drinkable. We saw off at least half of the remaining bottle before we were joined by Fred.

'Have some of this,' Tiny encouraged Fred, whilst putting his arm around him in a 'You know, you are my best mate' fashion. Fred sniffed the concoction, held it up to the light and said, 'Fuck off, that's meths!'

Tiny then also held it up to the light again, confirmed it was a lilac purple colour, sniffed it, nodded an agreement that Fred's analysis was correct, and then took another gulp from the bottle.

The following morning, we were all due to go downhill skiing. This meant getting on the coach at 9.00 am with quite remarkable hangovers that would, in different circumstances, put an African elephant out of action for days. The expectation of downhill skiing all day did make it all worthwhile. However, two hours on a coach full of hungover, farting and burping marines could not have made life pleasant for the driver. We arrived at the ski slope and donned our equipment, including bib-and-brace-style salopettes. We manoeuvred ourselves onto the ski lift and breathed in the freezing fresh air in the vain hope that it would be the cure for our hangovers. Tiny and I ascended the mountain on the lift in silence, with only the sound of skis compressing soft snow and the cable coming under tension as we passed each stanchion wheel.

As we neared the top of the slope, I felt a very uncomfortable stomach and bowel movement threatening a mass exodus of their contents. The sort of movement that requires some serious buttock-clenching, then a brisk walk to the loo, followed by a relieved sit down on the heads, with windows being flung open before you're sick in the sink.

I was, however, at the top of a mountain, with a 2-mile ski downhill towards the nearest heads at the cafe at the bottom of the slope. I had three layers of clothing on, and the depressing prospect of spending the rest of the day with my salopettes full of crap did not appeal. I set off like a man possessed. Both skis pointed straight down the slope as I took off over each lump and bump as gravity tried to overrule the efforts of my sphincter. Fortunately, no one else was on the slope because we had gotten there early. It would have made a nasty mess on impact if a young child had crossed my path at this time, both the blood on the snow and the brown mess in my underpants.

I skied right up to the outdoor toilet in the cold still air at the bottom of the slope, kicked my skis off and made a dash for the cubicle. Rather than the bottom falling out of my world, as would have been the case if I had not put in place years of Commando training on the record-breaking downhill run, it felt instead that the world was falling out of my bottom. The methylated spirits must have fermented my stomach contents; either that or I was sharing the cubicle with a two-week-old dead bear. I left the heads with the relief of a jumbo jet pilot having just had a near miss with another passenger plane. I sat down on a fence nearby and was joined by Tiny, as he casually skied up and sat next to me.

'You went a bit Banzai, Lou; we've got all day to go yet,' he said.

I explained my previous discomfort and indicated towards the heads cubicle that I considered out of bounds until the air cleared.

We then spent an enjoyable half-hour together, drinking coffee and tittering as skiers approach the cubicle, only to meet the invisible wall of fug that I had left behind.

As they searched for another less-pungent cubicle, they looked at the offending construction as if they had just slammed the door on a ravenous chained-up beast.

FULL BACKUP FROM SENIOR MANAGEMENT

These days it is fairly rare to find someone in management who will unswervingly demonstrate support for an individual or team when the task that was set for them starts to unravel, or through some unforeseen circumstance goes off course and could be heading for disaster. Managers are always covering their arse or that of the organization. This tends to lead to a distancing of the manager from anything controversial, or a system of barriers and bureaucracy before anything actually ever gets done. The responsibility of a task is spread around the workforce and the risk is pushed down to middle managers, who know their heads will roll if the boss's idea now goes wrong. Worse still is the boss who never makes a mistake as they never make a decision.

Incompetence is no doubt the cause of many military disasters. If, for example, military intelligence in South-East Asia in 1941 had spotted the high number of Japanese soldiers passing their cycling proficiency and pumping up their bicycle tyres, they may have predicted that the main form of attack on Malaya and Singapore was going to be with the majority of the Japanese Army cycling down the Malay peninsula, and taking it from the least-defended landward side, rather than approaching from the sea and facing the wide assortment of large-calibre British guns pointing out to sea.

Other historic disasters could have been avoided by the right command being given at the most relevant time.

'Don't fire until you see the whites of their eyes' is a famous command and usually drops the front ranks of any wild, charging army brandishing sharply pointed disembowelling weaponry. However, it may be less successful when the order is given during the hours of darkness.

There is no doubt that some military disasters could have been averted if the risk had not been taken in the first place, but who can predict the outcome of the courage of a calculated or a morally correct risk? If Britain and its small Commonwealth forces, who were already hard-pressed and in retreat on all fronts, had not stepped in and assisted Greece during the Second World War, the British Army in that theatre would not have lost many of their men and the best part of their equipment when forced to evacuate first Greece, and then Crete, in the face of superior German forces. Additionally, the Royal Navy would not have lost many valuable ships sunk by the overwhelming air power of the Luftwaffe. Clearly, this was a military disaster.

However, it is rarely pointed out that this action by British troops and the Royal Navy meant that Hitler had to hold up Operation *Barbarossa* for two months in 1941 as he needed the full force of the Luftwaffe to have air superiority over Russian forces. He had planned to start the invasion in the essential dry weather of the spring so that his military vehicles could move over the Russian steppes without getting bogged down. German troops eventually reached the outskirts of Moscow in October, but as the winter months set in they became paralyzed by the extreme cold and deep snow drifts. They were forced to remain there, unable to retreat and unable to advance as supply lines were impassable. If Hitler had started the invasion two months earlier, Moscow would have been reached by August, before the winter, and Moscow would likely have fallen, as would Stalingrad. Russia would have been out of the war and Hitler could have turned all his attention – and forces – on Britain.

There are sometimes unknown advantages to taking a risk.

On the other hand, if Nelson had attended a course in modern-day management, as a result of a well-evidenced risk assessment, highlighting that the Royal Navy was outnumbered and that it could get rough around the Bay of Biscay in the autumn, he would not have been put to sea and would have avoided the risk of the Battle of Trafalgar. However, Britain would then likely have been invaded by the French and Spanish within months. If the Royal Navy had remained inactive and the French made good a landfall at Bognor Regis, anyone pointing a finger at Nelson would no doubt have had the risk assessment waved in their face, and Nelson would have justified his inaction.

Being a good military leader can require all sorts of character traits and management skills that civilians never dream of. The great tactician may not be the best person to be the first out of the landing craft. Likewise, the junior NCO, who is able to extract his troops from a difficult situation, may not have a clue about logistics. It takes all types, and it can just be luck that the right type of leader is in the right place at the right time.

Royal Marines do try to make their own luck by ensuring high standards throughout the Corps. And one way a commander can engender the respect of the men is by showing reckless courage.

This can, however, end in tears, such as the commander in the American Civil War who is reported to have stood up from behind the ramparts where his men were taking shelter, and not firing back, and shouted encouragingly, 'They won't hit us from th...', falling dead with part of his skull removed by the accurate musket fire.

One of our company commanders in 42 Commando made a similar, but less famous, reckless speech. In training and on section battle attacks, we were always trained to only take cover if we were 'under effective enemy fire'. This is defined as bullets landing around your feet or men falling over beside you.

As L Company assaulted Mount Harriet during the advance on Stanley in the Falklands campaign, the lead troop came under fire and was held up. The company commander and his fire control party approached the area where the company was pinned down. Having assessed the situation, the company commander chose his words carefully.

It's a once-in-a-military career event when a leader has a chance to say inspiring words whilst under fire. No doubt remembering the American general on Omaha Beach on D-Day – who is quoted as saying, 'The only men who stay on this beach are dead men and those that are going to die' – the company commander stood up and announced loudly to those sheltering in the rocks around him, 'I don't call this effective enemy fire! Follow me!'

He then leapt to his feet, followed by the fire control party, who stood up more cautiously. The radio operator and the company second-in-command were both immediately raked with very effective enemy fire through both legs and dropped to the ground severely wounded. The whole fire control party, including the company commander, took cover in the rocks, nervously exchanging glances with the lead troop already taking cover. It was the wrong time to say, 'I told you so.' It was going to take more than inspirational words to encourage those marines to restart the advance up the mountain as bullets whined and bounced off the rocks just above their heads, and tracer rounds flashed past just inches in front of their noses, cracking and thumping as the short bursts pinned them down.

Despite the overwhelming threat to their own lives, the sheltering marines gave lifesaving first aid to the casualties. Entry and exit wounds were located, first field dressings were applied and tourniquets tightened to prevent the blood from pumping out.

They waited for their moment, and as soon as the hidden machine gunner had switched targets, they heroically hauled themselves to their feet and continued the advance into what felt like almost certain death, the company commander still leading from the front.

Meanwhile, on another part of the same mountain, Lieutenant Colonel Vaux, the CO of 42 Commando, stood on a fixed point in the open, boots braced on some exposed round boulders, silhouetted against the night-time flash of the exploding naval and artillery shells crashing into the enemy positions not more than 300 metres away. Standing upright and on a slightly lower rock looking to his front was the Forward Observation Officer (FOO), calmly calling in mortar, artillery and naval gunfire as tracer rounds passed their heads, striking rocks around them and careening off into the distant night. The CO hauled on the taut cable of the radio attaching him to his radio operator so that he could get the microphone end closer to his mouth. Frustrated by his lack of success, he glanced down towards the other end of the cable. He was almost surprised to see the radio operator crouched down amongst the rocks, also concentrating on the sending and receiving of crucial messages on the net, but in an obviously more sensible and far safer position than both the FOO and himself.

'I need some more slack,' the CO requested urgently.

'It's a bit dangerous up there, Sir,' the corporal pointed out.

The CO looked around at the lines of tracers curving towards his position, relented, and moved closer to his operator. The CO remained out in the open throughout the eight-hour night battle, on many occasions more exposed to death and injury than the leading sections. He was determined to command the assault to the very best of his mortal ability and make sure that all the assets available to him could generate the maximum yield of violence towards the enemy, thereby preventing and extinguishing any glimmer of hope that the Argentinian defenders had of holding that brutal mountain.

After the battle, he realized that he had not fired a single shot from his fully loaded rifle, slung over his shoulder and carried all the way up the mountain. He later reflected that he had been concentrating so much on winning the battle that it had not even entered his mind to use his own weapon. He was an inspiring example of true leadership. His bravery and leadership were his own admirable qualities; his luck and survival came from somewhere else.

Meanwhile, Lieutenant Colonel Whitehead, in charge of 45 Commando on the feature of Two Sisters next to Mount Harriet, was showing equal leadership qualities. An oppo of mine was with Zulu Company, assaulting the feature. Again, momentum was critical – keep moving forward, fire and manoeuvre, with 66mm LAWs rockets being fired at bunkers, grenades thrown and accurate artillery fire coming in. The whole of Zulu Company was shouting 'Zulu, Zulu!' as the assault gradually made progress and the enemy was dislodged.

The feature was a challenge to attack and an ideal position to defend. Captain Gardiner (of parade ground horse fame, now promoted to X-Ray Company of 45 Commando) stated, 'Royal Marines would have died of old age if they were defending Two Sisters.'

My friend had seen his oppos killed and seriously wounded on the mountainside during the initial part of the assault, and was not quite so enthusiastic to be point man of point section, as the assault continued. There was no question of not supporting his mates, and he certainly was not going to let them down, at any cost. He and his section were merely resting a short while as he sat on a rock and did up his boots in the deepest gulley, giving them the best cover from the chaos going on around them. They were waiting for the artillery to become a bit more effective and quieten down the well-supplied enemy machine gunners.

The battle raged on, artillery crashing in as para flares illuminated the whole mountainside. Lieutenant Colonel Whitehead and his fire control party yomped past, calling in more firepower onto selected targets. Seeing the section taking cover, he walked up to my oppo, slapped him on the back and shouted above the noise in his Home Counties accent, 'Well done, Sutcliffe, you're playing a blinder.'

The fire control party moved on into the danger zone, with rounds flying around their ears and mortar shells landing close by. The section rallied and moved up with the CO, having reloaded their weapons and cocked a few more 66mm anti-tank rockets, their eyes wild with the heat of battle.

Two years later, on a tour of Northern Ireland, K Company were again in the thick, spending the six-month tour in Crossmaglen (known as XMG). This was 'bandit country'. Everything was flown in by helicopter – rations, men and even cleaners. The roads were too dangerous to travel on by vehicle, many a squaddie having met his fate in the small village square, and the surrounding countryside, through well-planted bobby traps or ambush. Until our tour, the RUC had refused to patrol with the army for a while. As our tour progressed and the professionalism was shown on the ground, the RUC restarted joint patrols after an absence of five years.

The unit we took over from had lost three men, and the unit after us lost two. This number killed on a tour was considered low by XMG standards. We had a few close scrapes, but came home without losing a single man. We were firm but fair on vehicle checkpoints (VCPs), talking nicely to the occupants of cars whilst ensuring the vehicle was covered by a cocked GPMG. We got off helicopters 3 miles away from the VCP and yomped in, cutting our way through bushes and snipping the barbed wire on top of 6ft-tall stone walls. The cows in South Armagh must have been pretty athletic! We never used the same gap twice, and the first thing the locals knew about our VCP was when we emerged from bushes at the roadside and put the caltrops (spiked chains) across the road. At a given time, the VCP was packed up and we disappeared into the countryside, again taking a different route to a different pickup point.

On one such patrol, a sniping occurred. The patrol was lucky and the target was missed, but the 'crack and thump' of the bullet passing between two of the patrol assisted in identifying the firing point, and the sniper was pinged. After that, the radio came to life with, 'Contact, wait out.'

The patrol called in backup, who immediately and successfully assaulted the firing point, killing one terrorist, and also reported that they may have seen another running away, sending a burst of GPMG and LMG (light machine gun) fire after him.

The follow-up operation was put into action, but with the firing point being so close to the border, the chances were that the other gunman had got away. The patrol remained on the ground for several hours, fully aware that when they got back to XMG, they were going to be grilled by the intelligence unit and the RUC to check all was in order and that the killing of the sniper, intent on murdering one of the patrols, was lawful.

The 21-year-old corporal and his even younger patrol arrived back at XMG by helicopter. There, waiting on the helipad, was the commanding officer. As the patrol stepped out of the door of the Lynx helicopter, the CO shook each member of the patrol by the hand and patted them on the back as they walked past towards the debriefing room. The CO walked with the corporal and was seen congratulating him on a job well done as they disappeared behind the blast walls surrounding the accommodation block.

If there was any doubt in the patrol's minds as to the backup and support they were about to receive from senior management, it was dispelled on the helipad.

FURTHER 'TAILS' OF
NORTHERN IRELAND

Wherever soldiers go in the world, you can guarantee that if based in any place for longer than a few days, somehow a stray dog will turn up and get befriended, fed, generally made a fuss of and sometimes even taken home and adopted by one of the marines after the tour.

Northern Ireland was no different. Within weeks of the start of our tour of South Armagh in 1984, a number of dogs were found hanging around, taking advantage of any dropped titbits of offered treats. They would gain the confidence of the unstimulated soldier and an ancient bond would start that meant food and security for the dog, with companionship and an early warning system against predators and other unknown dangers for the soldiers.

Some units even handed over dogs almost as part of the inventory of a security base or secure airfield. Some dogs knew when they were onto a good thing, making themselves comfortable on a well-worn, but still usable, pusser's armchair, claiming it as their own and covering it in dog hair. Dog hair would then adhere to any visitor who made the mistake of sitting on the dog's chair in the waiting room.

Senior RUC officers waiting to fly down to Keady or Forthill, to brief their isolated police colleagues, would invariably appear at the helipad waiting room and make a coffee from the 'makings' on a nearby shelf. Then they would look around for the nearest chair, awaiting the arrival of their helicopter and a lift. Unbeknownst to them, the yellow Labrador, who could hear the distant sound of the approaching helicopter long before a human was able to, had only just vacated his favourite spot to go outside and bark at the helicopter as it approached for landing. The helicopter would come in low, just clearing the trees before banking around to land on the helipad and quickly pick up the day's passengers.

As the RUC officers put down their half-drunk coffee cups and picked up their weapons and briefcases, they could be seen smiling and looking at the backs of their trousers, brushing off all the dog hair from their dark green uniforms that had just the right weave to pick up a furry coat like velcro.

Once the Labrador had done his duty, and the helicopter had been welcomed in and out again with some further unnecessary barking, he would make his way purposely back to his chair to wearily climb back on board and curl up with a deep huff of breath. A sniff of the seat would confirm that a pair of RUC trousers had recently been sitting in HIS chair. Maybe they left some crisps down the side of the chair, in which case a quick sniff around might be rewarded with a tasty snack.

Some dogs really worked for their keep. A black Labrador, with fox-like cleverness, decided to attach himself to the detachment manning the Sangers[16] sited on the hills overlooking the border. These Sangers and lookout posts had sophisticated CCTV and camera equipment that could zoom onto a car's registration plate from over a mile away. (Not too impressive with today's technology, but this was 1984 and such a sophisticated lens was then only used by the military and the best wildlife photographers.) The capability of these cameras was actually a military secret.

Sandbagged walls were in place on some outposts, but most relied on their high and isolated strategic viewpoint for protection. They were at their most vulnerable from a night attack. It wasn't a big leap of the imagination to figure out that some well-motivated terrorist could sneak up at night and plant a small device underneath the sleeping quarters. They could then quietly make their escape back into the darkness and detonate it at a tactical distance, using a remote control or a timer switch, and cross the border a few minutes later into Southern Ireland and almost certain safety from pursuit, leaving death, injury and destruction to the occupants of the lookout post.

---

16. A Sanger is a temporary fortified position with a breastwork, originally constructed with stones, sandbags, gabions or similar materials. Sangers are normally constructed in terrain where the digging of a trench is not possible.

To counteract this, sentries remained on guard all night, equipped with superb night-vision goggles in addition to the pink Mark 1 listening devices on the sides of their heads (i.e., their ears).

The black Lab who was affectionately named 'Fleabag' would choose to sleep each night underneath the sleeping area. This gave us all a greater sense of protection. On some nights, Fleabag would stir and move over to where the sentry was located and stare into the darkness, sniffing the air, with his ears raised to pick up the slightest sound. Not barking or whining, just staring. This would put the wind up some sentries, but certainly focused them, and alertness was raised as eyes were pressed to night sights with greater zealousness, covering likely areas of approach.

Some sections would even 'stand to' if Fleabag started to stare into the night. All would quietly and efficiently take up all-around defence, with thumbs on the safety catch of their weapon, loaded and made ready.

Fleabag was seen as too much of an asset for someone to adopt and take home, so as far as I am aware he continued his watch non-stop, on duty until he died. This outpost was never attacked once during the whole period of 'the troubles'.

Other terrier-type dogs were taken on patrol from various security bases. They used to start trembling when they heard the helicopter approaching about three minutes away, long before we heard it. This was also very useful when the patrol was to be extracted from the middle of the countryside. When the terrier started to tremble, the patrol knew it was time to pick up their kit, have a last check all around and standby to run out to the prearranged LZ from the laying-up point in a bush. An approaching helicopter was equivalent to an owner shaking a dog lead and saying, 'Walkies.'

One of these terriers used to get so excited that he would jump up at the helicopter as it came in to land and try to bite the tyres. This was good for a laugh as far as it went, but if you had a new crew who were not used to a dog jumping up at them, they would sometimes hover and refuse to land until one of us picked up the wriggling creature and tucked him inside a combat jacket.

Another faithful brindle-coloured mongrel, who was cruelly named 'Piss Face', would patrol the hedge line parallel to the route of the patrol. Some of these hedges were too thick to get through, so another pair of eyes connected to a keen nose was a welcome addition. Piss Face also 'volunteered' to run through culverts ahead of the patrol. It was common practice for the local terrorist active service unit to plant bombs in these underground water pipes and ditches and detonate them as a foot patrol or security force vehicle passed over.

The dog could be seen going in one end and emerging from the other, then going back through the tunnel again, and would dash back and seem to report back to the patrol, indicating that it was safe to proceed. He was praised and given treats of chocolate or half the contents of a freshly opened tin of bacon grill from one of the patrol's rations. This keen collie-like dog was always happy to join in with any group of marines sitting with their backs against a stone wall having a drink of tea, eagerly sharing any AB biscuits with meat paste spread. But as soon as the AB biscuit was wolfed down, he did not wait around for unnecessary stroking or affection. Instead, he would make a tactical beeline for the highest upwind ground to start a clearance patrol of the area the soldiers were resting in, only casting a sideways glance at the sentries already in position, as if to check that they were doing their job correctly so as to keep everyone safe. Again, not one patrol that had Piss Face along was ever bombed or attacked.

If you were able to take a bit of time out from the harsh reality of the whole mess that contributed towards the Northern Ireland situation, you could see why canine legends were built up around these relationships between man and dog during the shared strains of combat operations.

Maybe they were the reincarnated souls of youthful soldiers who had their promising young lives snatched away suddenly, deliberately and violently by some self-justifying evil that had become deeply engrained into the psyche of a few misguided and inadequate individual residents in that small, rain-swept Emerald Isle.

That life force and spirit was looking after other young lives with an unstinting devotion and the promise of the other half of the tin of bacon grill.

Piss Face was taken home to Hull by the company stores Colour Sergeant and adopted by a new family, with – fortunately for him – a new name.

NEGLIGENT DISCHARGE

A Negligent Discharge (ND) is nothing rude or premature. It's the official title for when a weapon goes off accidentally; or more accurately, when the user presses the trigger by mistake.

I remember that when we had our pre-Northern Ireland training in 1984, one of the lectures was about this subject. The instructor used a list of statistics gathered during the 1970s and early 1980s to frighten us all.

List of NDs in Northern Ireland from 1968–1983
Self-Loading Rifles – 1256
GPMGs – 248
Pistols – 3,005 (this one was surprising, being that most of the soldiers carried rifles!)
SMGs – 178
84mm anti-tank weapon – 1

The Light Infantry sergeant delighted in telling us the well-known story of the only 84mm ND in Ireland.

A young officer (YO), keen to keep his men occupied and fully up to speed, decided that instead of normal rifle or machine gun weapons training, he would update the men on the 84mm Karl Gustav anti-tank weapon. This beast weighed in at 36lb and could take out a Russian T72 tank. And when it was fired, the operators felt like they had been blown up as well.

The YO instructed one of the old hands to go to the stores and collect some practice rounds. The old hand questioned the YO about this and asked, 'Are you sure you want me to get practice rounds, Sir?'

The YO took this as insubordination, and so as to stamp his authority on the troop, he repeated his request, making it an order.

'Right 'O, Sir,' the old hand confirmed. 'Practice rounds it is then.'

The 84mm has a number of rounds. There are the live green and yellow high-explosive rounds, the inert drill rounds and the Target Practice Tracer Projectile (TPTP) rounds. The latter round does not have an explosive warhead, but it does have the full charge to send the round at high-velocity speed into practice targets on ranges.

Marine Suggs had been ordered to get the practice rounds, so that was what he was going to get.

He returned about fifteen minutes later, much to the disgust of the YO, who had been filling in time talking about Russian tank recognition as his audience's eyes gradually glazed over.

'OK, Marine Suggs, you're the Number 1. Marine Maxwell, you're Number 2.' Then, to add realism to the scenario, the officer shouted, 'Enemy tank 300 at 12 o'clock! Come on Suggs, get hold of that weapon; load, cock it, take aim and fire!'

'Are you sure, Sir?' Marine Suggs questioned his decision-making yet again.

'Of course I am. Now fire the bloody weapon, the tank is almost on you.'

'OK, Sir,' he replied, and with this, the portacabin that the weapon training was taking place in erupted. With a back blast danger area of 40 metres the TPTP had no trouble in removing the end of the portacabin behind the firing point, as well as the door on the side. The TPTP round went out of the other end of the hut and straight in between the top and bottom bunks of the accommodation hut next door, where off-duty marines were sleeping, drilling neat 84mm holes as it went through all the walls. The round continued on across West Belfast housing estates and towards the security base, where 2 Para were based, and lodged itself in a nearby house.

The dust settled in the remains of the portacabin as the quick reaction force and all available helicopters took off. Blokes came out cocking SLRs from nearby barrack rooms, dressed just in their trousers, expecting to defend the security base from the enemy, who by the sounds of it were already in the backyard.

The now-deaf Marine Suggs grinned to himself as he looked innocently at the YO, raising his eyebrows in veiled surprise.

'You did say practice round, didn't you, Sir?'

Within half an hour, all had returned to normal, apart from the training portacabin and the hearing of the 84mm training party. The blokes in the cabin next door were also a bit twitchy and were having trouble getting back to sleep.

A telex then arrived in the guardroom from 2 Para, requesting the use of the Royal Marines' 84mm indoor range.

FULL BOARD AND A FULL WALLET

It was November 1984 and we had missed the summer by spending it in South Armagh, getting rained on. It had been hot and we had spent a lot of time out of doors, but we were still pasty white. Cam cream, several layers of combats and security bases with no windows had caused the feeling of vitamin D deficiency.

We also had a female deficiency. I knew it was bad when, three months into the tour, I had lusted after the dental Wren just before the dentist had drilled one of my teeth. Whilst still in pain and swilling my mouth out, she bent forward and I got a view of her ample cleavage. She caught me looking and just coyly smiled. It was the closest encounter I'd had in six months, and she was a large girl with modest good looks. I had disturbed dreams about her for several nights. Well, I was only 22 and was not sure how to play it with mysterious and out-of-my-league 24-year-old dental Wrens.

The next day I visited Armagh barracks, where it was rumoured that sixteen Wrens were based. Sixteen to 258 blokes were still better odds than one visiting dental Wren chaperoned at all times by a bearded bloke with needles and drills at Bessbrook Barracks.

I met up with a good mate of mine called Burt, a driver based at Armagh who also came from my hometown. That evening we went up to the NAAFI and had a few beers. Life was different in the Armagh Barracks bars, as they had some women and daylight in the barracks. You did, however, have to put up with the Ulster Defence Regiment, as it was their bar. Some engaged you in conversation, which was mainly based on their bigoted view of 'the troubles'. It all became a bit depressing within a short space of time. They were obviously going to talk about nothing else and assumed wrongly that we all had the same views because we also wore green. When you go someplace in the world and spend months of your life trying to keep the peace, and genuinely try to make things better or at least keep the lid on it, it comes as a moment of disappointed realization when you meet such characters, as some were in the UDR at that time. You realize that you and all those who have gone before you are pissing in the wind, a wind generated by small-minded people from small-minded estates and villages who refuse to give an inch. Both sides had the same extremists who refused to change.

Anyway, 'bollocks to them', I thought. I was with a good mate and having a beer in a bar.

I told Burt about my minor encounter with the dental nurse, to which his ears pricked up.

'Oh, Cheryl, you mean. I've been shagging her for the past two months,' Burt stated with such nonchalance between puffs on his fag, that it was obviously true.

I took another sip of my beer and looked into the bottom of the glass, feeling that a full-blown outburst was appropriate. Burt had been with the fantasy woman of my dreams and I was still in the land of frustrated make-believe where a coy smile meant that she fancied me, and given the right circumstances, without the dentist present, I would be in there. I chose to be mature and just fume jealously to myself.

The tour was completed without so much as a sniff. I didn't even get a visit from my dental Wren again; she was probably playing hard to get. Anyway, she had been soiled by Burt, so I wouldn't have, even if she had begged me.

Burt travelled home on leave in my car after the Ireland tour. He slept most of the way home, not surprising really when he had been bonking the dental Wren for most of the tour. He must have been looking upon leave as a bit of a rest. He snored contently in between me waking him up to ask if we were going the right way, just to disturb him on the very familiar route home.

Burt was a good friend but he had bloody annoyed me by taking liberties with my passenger seat, sleeping and handing out sweets in a thoughtful manner. The bastard even paid for the petrol and the sandwiches on the way home. How could I convey my annoyance to him, having realized that he had just taken his chances and it had all worked out well for him? Maybe I just needed to talk normally to the next Wren I fancied rather than just saying nothing.

On the first day on leave in England, the weather was so miserable that we booked a holiday to 'somewhere in the sun'. We booked Tenerife. Seventy degrees on average, lots of sun, and maybe parties of dental Wrens also flying out. We knew some other blokes in the company were going there as well, so we arranged to meet up in Playa De Las Americas, but thought we could operate better if just a pair, so just one evening meet-up maybe.

We arrived at our four-star hotel and I knew instantly that it was a good idea to book the trip. Whilst we slowly got ready to go out that first evening, I sat on the balcony taking in the sun and the view. With a personal stereo on, listening to 'Do You Know the Way to San Jose' by Frankie Goes to Hollywood, I was lapping it up. Palm trees formed a backdrop to an inviting swimming pool. With the sun low in the sky, I could feel the warmth on my face as my body absorbed the rays like a sponge. The feeling of being in the sun for the first time in months is enhanced when you have just missed a summer out. The experience of lazing around a pool is further enhanced when you have a self-belief that you deserve it. The bank account needed venting as well; as usual, I had spent sod all in Ireland. I was in good company and due to meet some more mates the following evening. I was going through one of those 'glad I joined up' moments.

Without me realizing it, the dental Wren disappeared from my mind. The first coy smile from any one of the scantily dressed 'parties' in the bars on the island, and I would be in there tonight.

The week progressed and we met up with two girls staying at our hotel. They were in their twenties too, but their Mum was with them and had paid for the holiday. Burt charmed both the Mum and the best-looking daughter, and Mum seemed to like us both and allowed us to chat with them all, buying drinks and ice creams for them. The afternoons were spent laying around the pool with the girls, and as the week progressed I got on well with the other daughter.

Burt then found out that the older daughter was engaged to be married and that this was a bit of a girls' hen holiday just before the marriage.

Oh dear, poor Burt, and there was me getting on so well with her single sister! We got on so well, in fact, that regular walks down to the beach were made, which diverted to mine and Burt's room. I don't think the engaged sister approved, and Mum certainly wouldn't have. Evenings were spent with Burt and I going out early, getting drunk and then meeting up with the girls when they had finally got themselves ready. We knew that when we met up with our mates we would be accused of 'going welfare' with these two girls, and no doubt they would get some stick. But we just went with the flow, expecting to meet up with them at some time in one of the local haunts. They were a nice family and it was great to have some normality after six months in NI.

We still hadn't met up with the other lads, who were supposed to be at the same location, and assumed we had got the wrong week. On our last night, we went to a place called Los Christianos for a change. The place is now as overdeveloped as everywhere else in Tenerife, but then it seemed a bit dull, with only three bars and one small club. We were just about to get a taxi back to Playa when the bar we were in was invaded by twelve drunken blokes wearing matching togas. Not only did their togas match each other's, but they also matched the curtains in the bar and the hotel reception. They came in like a right bunch of arses, as if they owned the place, gobbing off and laughing loudly. It took a few moments to register that these were our friends from 42 Commando!

They were all howling drunk, and immediately upon seeing us, felt the need to shout incoherently as loudly as possible whilst pointing at us just to indicate to everyone in the bar that we knew them. They then enveloped us in a rugby-type scrum of beery breath and body odour. (Of course, if the roles were reversed we would surely have been witty and amusing and not the pain in the arse that this lot was rapidly becoming.) To reassure us, some of the group put their arms around us and slurred, 'You know what, you're my best mate you are', as we succumbed to smelly horrible blokes.

The girls thinned out pretty quickly and got in a taxi to anywhere other than the bar we were in.

Burt, having grandparents from India, had no problems catching a healthy sun tan. I was in the stage of changing from a lobster shade of red to a subtle 'too long under the sun lamp' look. These blokes were all still as pasty as the day they had landed, and they had been there one day longer than us.

We were then told the sad and sorry tale of how on the first night they had all gone out on a 'silly rigs' (i.e., fancy dress) run, dressed as Hawaiian hula girls, when one of their gang had befriended a civvy at the bar who had one of these new camcorders. A civil conversation was struck up by all accounts, which resulted in Sutty borrowing the gentleman's camera for some 'what's underneath the hula skirt' shots. Only he dropped it and it broke. The civvy decided that the best way to deal with this was to punch Sutty in the mouth. Quite reasonable in the circumstances.

One thing led to another and the civvy's mates joined in, and they got filled in. The bar staff tried to intervene, but they got filled in. The bouncers joined in, and they got filled in too. The local unarmed police arrived, and they also got filled in. The armed national police force arrived, they drew their batons and pistols, and suddenly it all went quiet.

The national police jumped to the right conclusion that they had a right bunch of troublemakers in their quiet community who needed to be taught a lesson, and promptly put them in the local jail overnight. The following morning, the local magistrate considered all the evidence and also concluded that he had a bunch of troublemakers in his community who needed to be taught a lesson, and promptly returned them all to jail for seven days. This would take them up to the night before their flight home.

They told us that the jail had been like something from the film *Midnight Express*. Everyone had to crap in a communal bucket, there was poor food and no access to any solicitors. They had a visit from the British Consulate, who seemed to think that the commanding officer would be most interested in their plight, rather than trying to see their version of events and give some poignant legal advice. Their impression was that the only place they would find sympathy with any officials was in the dictionary.

Whilst in jail, they said that the police had thrown someone into the cell one night with a bullet wound. This person had stolen a car and run off before being stopped by a 9mm round in the shoulder. One of the marines, Knocker, was able to give him some first aid that night before he went to the hospital the following afternoon.

As the evening progressed at Los Christianos, we became aware of large numbers of national police outside the bar looking in. Some were tapping their batons in a casual but menacing manner, while others were checking the quick-release clip on their 9mm pistols. No further incidents were reported that night.

Meanwhile, in the bar, Sutty was keen to show me his face, on which, when viewed under the right light, one could clearly see the outlines of prison window bars where he had spent his seven days pining, looking out of the only window in the communal cell facing the sun.

DO I STAY OR DO I GO NOW?

The Corps is a constantly changing organization with a huge turnover of personnel. There are about 7,000 Royal Marines in the Corps, and during the 1980s there were about 1,000 new recruits put through the system each year. By no means did they all pass out of training, but this does indicate the numbers required to keep the Corps up to strength. Most people see the Royal Marines as a short-term career, with the vast majority doing three to five years. A significant number then leave after nine years. I remember a talk on internal recruitment once indicating that only about 2 per cent of initial recruits stay for the full twenty-two years.

This tended to build a culture of 'the grass being greener on the other side'. Success stories would be spread around of an ex-Booty (i.e., Royal Marine) who had made it good setting up their own business, or who had left the Corps to become a Mountie in Canada, or married a rich woman in Australia. Others saw the civilian police or fire service in the UK as an attractive career. At that time, police forces had a drive to recruit ex-servicemen. The pay and conditions were better, and you got to go home at the end of the shift rather than some grotty security base in Northern Ireland, where you had another four months to go before your two weeks of Easter leave.

This was the situation I found myself in 1983. Many of my mates were leaving the Corps for pastures new. Bill was joining the Metropolitan Police, while Mark, a friend I travelled home with on most periods of leave, was leaving due to a new wife and young family. The Corps was in flux and I seemed to be the only one who had not put in his ticket to leave, or 'go outside' as it was termed.

The year of 1983 started with the usual Norway trip and a rumour that we may have a Canada trip in the summer. This encouraged me to stay for that year, but I did put my eighteen-month notice in to leave in 1984. The timing was perfect: summer in Canada, another winter in Norway – with loads of local overseas allowance – and then join The Met or seek my fortune in some foreign land that would no doubt welcome with open arms a 21-year-old ex-marine with a qualification in carpentry and a half-baked idea of setting himself up in business.

Upon return from the regular Norway trip, there were a few more conquests notched up on the Norwegian wooden bedpost. My pockets were going 'jingly jangly' with all the money that a single bloke could earn in a cold climate with very warm-hearted people. An understanding MOD, with a realistic attitude to the cost of living, meant the local overseas allowance was £10 a day for a young marine, with full board and lodgings paid for. Added to this was free downhill skiing at the weekends, the greatest expense being the coffee in the ski cafe. Life was not so bad, but I needed to make a few decisions about my future career and life.

This was helped by the unexpected opportunity of a trip on the Corps yacht to France in May, a summer maintenance party to Norway in June, the Canada trip in July and the chance to take all the leave I had missed on a road trip around America in August. Things were looking up, but I considered that the eighteen-month notice was still a good idea. It also seemed a reasonably long period of time in which to make up my mind.

Time, however, ticks by.

The Norwegian summer maintenance party was a new one for me. The brief was that fifteen of us would fly to the camp where some of the units had stayed during the winter and put the wooden buildings back in order for the following winter's deployment. There were also 'wombling duties' to perform, such as picking up gash and other rubbish left on exercise areas that had been hidden by the snow, which had now all melted. This kept the locals happy and prevented land owners from putting in exaggerated claims to the MOD for rubbish left on their land by marines on winter exercise. It was a cost-effective way of carrying out this maintenance, we were told, due to the high costs of Norwegian tradesmen. (I think it prevented the MOD from getting ripped off yet again by some local shark or council.)

We would be staying in the Elvegardsmoen officers' mess building, with a good egg of a Captain QM in charge, who had arranged plenty of good victuals and a large stock of duty-free goods with which to assist successful party planning and, of course, to be used as an essential tool for bartering with the locals.

Darby Allen was our Colour Sergeant, who was supposed to arrange the maintenance schedule and keep us in good order. Darby, or 'Colours' as we all respectfully referred to him, was old school but fairly laid back; so long as the work got done, he didn't mind a bit of pratting around.

We were there for a month in a beautiful country where the sun does not set in the summer. We were on a generous local overseas allowance, and between Darby and the QM, we had a good officer and SNCO who weren't going to get too heavy. As ever, we quickly established healthy and unhealthy contacts with the locals, this being a small town in northern Norway that had 600 marines visit each winter. We were only fifteen, with a fairly strong backup in the duty-free department and our own self-sufficient setup to take full advantage of and kick the arse out of wherever possible.

Narvik was the closest and only city, and we quickly found the local haunts and enjoyed the atmosphere of this city within the Arctic Circle, where you could drink all day and night and it never got dark. When you leave a venue at 3 o'clock, you're not sure if it's 3.00 pm or 3.00 am. A girl I met up with informed me that the only way to tell if it was early morning or mid-afternoon was to observe the local people: 'If they are drunk, it's 3.00 am, if they are sober, it's 3.00 pm.'

Narvik was some 30km from Elvegardsmoen, and transport was required to get between the two locations. It was the norm for friendly locals to meet you for the first time, and after a conversation, offer a lift for the 60km round-trip if they were going that way. The Norwegian language course that some of us had taken came in handy on these occasions, as even though most locals spoke perfect English, I think they were aware that you were making an effort. This was the women as well as the men; some would put you up for the night after a party and then offer you the keys to their cars the morning after, so long as you brought it back the following night. There was no need to steal dumper trucks or buses to get back to camp in northern Norway.

Locally, the Bjorkvik Hotel was the place in which to be seen. Not the most exciting of venues, but it did have a bar and comfortable lounge area with a jukebox that played all of Slim Whitman's best 1950s hits.

Being a more mature and sensible type, Darby refused to venture out to the fleshpots of Narvik and preferred to stay at the Bjorkvik Hotel. One evening, Jim and I missed the transport to Narvik so decided to have a look at the local hotel. We met up with Darby and the QM, who coincidently had met up with his 'winter wife', which could have explained his enthusiasm for these summer maintenance trips. The QM made his excuses and left with his 'friend'.

Darby was, as usual, smartly dressed in a shirt and tie, with his slightly longer than regulation Teddy Boy hairstyle Brylcreemed back, polished shoes and smartly pressed trousers. He remained with us for the evening, spinning stories about when the Corps really used to go to interesting places, like Singapore and Hong Kong. We also mentioned how good it must have been doing those Gallipoli landings in a steam pinnace, to which we received a satisfactory, 'Fuck off!' This indicated that he had understood the joke and acknowledged that he was an 'old git', but that he wasn't going to bite.

We had a few more beers than we should have had and wandered out into the daylight, thinking about how we were going to get a lift back to camp. We had little luck. Maybe at 2.00 am, the locals in Elvegardsmoen were not so keen on giving three drunken marines a lift back the 5km to camp. Or maybe the 600 marines on the wintertime deployment had buggered up the lift situation. Either way, it looked as if we were going to have to yomp back, and so started out. Jim then went for a call of nature behind a roadside building and came back with two bicycles and a big grin on his face.

'Guess who's OIC [Officer In Charge] transport tonight,' he announced proudly, mounting the best of the two bikes and heading off at speed, whilst leaving the one with the fitted shopping rack dumped at our feet as if he had presented us with the ultimate answer to our current pedestrian situation.

Not being one to look a gift horse in the mouth, I mounted the ladies' shopping cycle, confidently told Darby to sit astride the shopping rack behind me and started to pedal after Jim, who was already around the first corner of the dirt track.

We had some catching up to do.

The track ran alongside a fast-flowing river and wound its way back up a steep valley in the general direction of the camp.

I remember looking down at Darby's black polished shoes and neat creases in his trousers as I attempted to keep my feet on the pedals as we picked up speed and weaved to avoid puddles. Darby hung on nervously, encouraging me with the words, 'If you put me in the river, Lew, you are on galley fatigue party for the rest of the trip.'

I assured Darby that I was an expert cyclist and that I wasn't all that drunk anyway, in a non-too-convincing manner. Darby had, after all, bought one-third of the beer we had just quaffed.

Ahead of me, I could see Jim cycling along, head down, bike weaving from side to side as he peddled as hard as he could. He disappeared around a corner and I thought all was lost and that he would be back to camp ages before we arrived. But as we rounded the corner, Jim was at the trackside, cursing and swearing at his bike, his hands covered in black oil as he tried to put the chain on again. As we passed him at breakneck speed, even Darby whooped a triumphant cry as he too became caught up in the stupid rivalry of drunken people racing borrowed bikes along a Norwegian dirt track in broad daylight at 2.00 am in the morning.

The next incline slowed us down, and I could hear Jim's manic laughter as, no doubt fully recovered from his unplanned pit stop, he rapidly made ground on us. We reached the brow of the hill and it was then all downhill to camp. Jim passed, taking the piss with a royal wave and a stupid drunken grin, and then took hold of the handlebars, stood up on the peddles and peddled like billy-oh for the finish line.

I watched Jim's back wheel snaking from side to side, lifting the dust as the tyre struggled to maintain a grip on the loose surface. The snaking became an uncontrolled speed wobble. Like a Spitfire fighter plane having lost its tail section, he soon spiralled out of control. Jim wrestled with the handlebars, all hope obviously lost, but still maintained a vice-like grip as the bike crashed onto its right-hand side and slid towards a large rhododendron bush marking the boundary of the road.

Jim and the bike hit a root and disappeared into the bush with a flurry of leaves and the noise of substantial branches being broken. A cloud of dust marked the spot where Jim had come unstuck, and I found the whole incident hilarious. Darby, having not witnessed Jim's impression of a crash test dummy, was not so amused. He was hanging on for dear life, having felt his trusty steed begin to wobble as the rider burst out laughing and took a course that seemed to be heading straight for the rhododendron bushes on the side of the road.

'For fuck's sake, Lew!' Darby cried as we parted the foliage of the bush at speed, right at the spot where the dust was still settling from Jim's efforts at stunt cycling.

I remember the front wheel catching in a lower branch and the feeling of flying through the air, hands clasped onto the now non-existent handlebars and my legs still peddling the thin air in a cross between my leg muscles remembering that they had just been peddling a bike and my survival instinct trying to get the landing gear down in time.

I landed on my back on the other side of a drainage ditch, with my legs in the crystal-clear water. All was quiet as I struggled to catch my breath from a severe winding.

Looking back, I could see the ladies' shopping bike hung up in the branches of the rhododendron bush. There was a rustle in the undergrowth and Jim came out of the bushes, crawling on his tummy towards me, with a stupid drunken grin fixed on his face. Branches had caused a number of scratches on his features, and he had leaves and bits of twig in his hair. He said nothing as he tried to spit out dust and dry leaves from his mouth.

Of Darby, nothing could be seen. I looked from the bike to the bush and to Jim – nothing! I then looked into the drainage ditch, and there, lying on his back at the bottom of the 3ft-deep water, was Darby. His eyes were open and he was making goldfish-like motions with his mouth as if he couldn't understand why he was having trouble breathing underwater. He surfaced and sat bolt upright, pond weed merged with his now unkempt rock-a-billy hairstyle, his tie having been severed in half, with the tell-tale signs of an oily cycle chain across his chest. He breathed in the life-giving oxygen and sat there stunned.

Jim and I dissolved into side-splitting laughter as Darby stood up and said, 'For fuck's sake, Lew, look at the state of my trousers.' This caused us further paralyzing mirth as Darby pulled long strands of pond weed out of his hair and tried to smooth his Elvis hairstyle back into place whilst he dripped, soaking wet, with his tattered tie hanging out to one side like a Biggles scarf.

'Fuck you two, I am walking back,' he announced, and yomped through the hole we had just made in the rhododendron bush, striding purposefully back to camp, leaving wet footprints in his wake. We met him back at the bar in the officers' mess, where he was already telling his side of the story before we got back and made him look foolish with our version.

Darby woke us up early the next morning and got us to load the bikes onto a truck, and we dropped them off quietly behind the house where we found them, quickly getting back in the truck and driving off.

As the month progressed, Darby continued to keep his own personal standards high, always turning out in a smartly pressed dress of the day with polished shoes, whilst the rest of us went for the more practical set of green overalls and pusser's 'steaming bats' (shoes with hardened toe caps).

We continued to get through the work schedule at, in Darby's opinion, an alarming rate. Each morning, we would fill up a 4-ton truck with roofing felt, bitumen and paint, and head off into the hills. We arranged the back of the 4-tonner with armchairs and tea-making facilities rather than the more traditional stark wooden and metal benches. Severely hung over, we would flop into the armchairs and have the run ashore debrief whilst bumping along to the location Darby had pointed to on the map, to slap paint and creosote all over the next set of Lyggen huts and nail some roofing felt onto any dodging looking roofs.

Darby kept a fine balance between keeping the QM happy with the work rate and doing his best to keep the standard of discipline just high enough for no one to get in the shit. He was concerned, however, with one of our party, Gilly.

Gilly had joined us from the Logistics Regiment. Upon first meeting him, you would form the opinion that he was either unhinged or desperate to seek attention. He had been seriously wounded in the Falklands. He explained that he had once been a very quiet young marine, but all this had changed when a bomb had landed next to him, killing several of his mates and severely wounding him in the groin and legs. He had gone to the BMA hospital on the beach and been repatriated to the UK, where he made a full physical recovery, but had since noticed certain behavioural problems.

Whilst employed on the daily working parties, he took to wearing his Sony Walkman earphones with the volume up full, and also insisted on wearing the issue goggles and dust mask. Gilly would sing at full voice whilst covering dozens of square metres per hour of weather-worn shiplap cladding with a 4in brush and a large bucket of creosote. This part of his work was fine as far as Darby was concerned. What worried Darby most was that Gilly had neatly painted a matching set of suspenders, stockings and a bra in white gloss paint on the green issue overalls that he wore each day.

Darby was more used to the established routine of UK camp life, where marines would turn to in three neatly spaced ranks with the odd button undone, thereby allowing the Colour Sergeant to fulfil his role and keeping standards high by pointing out such minor discrepancies on parade. He was not sure how to deal with this one.

After much turmoil, he used the tried-and-tested tactic of ignoring it and hoping that Gilly didn't do anything to drop himself, and therefore the whole detachment, in the shit during this short trip. He would be someone else's problem in the Logistics Regiment at the end of the month.

The Lyggen huts were spread over a wide area of our winter training ground, and each day we would head out to a different area, using our map-reading skills and initiative to get the job done as quickly as possible and make sure we were clear for a run ashore in the evening. On one such excursion, we arrived at an isolated location where there appeared to be only three lodges to paint and creosote. We were on a round-robin trip with an overnight stop in Harstad, so we didn't want to hang around. Jim came up with the idea of dropping two of us off at the three huts, whilst the rest moved on to the next larger area of lodges before returning to collect the pair after they had completed their task. Everyone agreed that this was a sound plan, so Gilly and Addy de-bussed with a small DIY store of equipment and started their task.

Jonno, the driver, continued navigating the way to the next location, where a hard day's work was put in and all tasks were completed to the usual slip-shod standard because Darby had stayed behind at Elvegardsmoen, knowing full well that another career-threatening run ashore was about to take place in Harstad that night.

Jonno picked up Gilly and Addy, leaving behind three huts smelling of fresh creosote, gloss paint and bitumen. Gilly mentioned something about a conversation he had had with a strange man whom he had been unable to get any sense out of, and who had appeared without warning, shouted something in Norwegian and then ran off. We concluded quietly that it must have been really strange behaviour for Gilly to recognize it as such.

We continued on with another run ashore until 3.00 am, still in broad daylight, getting a lift back to the camp in a North Sea trawler just setting off out to sea from Harstad harbour. Jim had used his Norwegian language course skills and the offer to buy some cod as a means to ask if the skipper wouldn't mind giving a few drunken, and potentially late, soldiers a ride home. Again, the natural Norwegian hospitality worked in our favour.

When we were dropped off at the pier head of the military camp, Jim ran up to the 4-tonner and returned with a bottle of whiskey for the crew. More cod was handed over in a plastic crate, and much waving and smiling continued until the fishing vessel chugged out of sight around the headland. Freshly fried cod for breakfast was followed by a bumpy ride back to Elvegardsmoen in the armchair express, feeling chuffed with ourselves as we had completed our tasks and had a week's supply of cod for the chef.

Upon arrival back at Elvegardsmoen, we were made aware that a local Norwegian Army liaison officer had called on the QM, voicing his concerns about the behaviour of the latest mobile working party. Apparently, a local farmer had been visiting three of his summer holiday homes and was disturbed to find that the colour had changed from a dull weather-worn grey to a dark oak creosote. This he did not mind too much; what had given him the real shock of his life was when he had rounded a corner and been confronted by a strange transvestite wearing a chemical and biological suit singing Abba's 'Dancing Queen' in full voice whilst no doubt decontaminating the surrounding area. The farmer was convinced that this was proof of the conspiracy theory that chemical warfare was being practised on his land by foreign troops, and that he had witnessed an undercover clean-up operation. The behaviour of the poor, affected transvestite soldier was conclusive, as far as he was concerned. All he wanted was fair compensation or he was going to the press!

All we wanted was a driver who could read a map and get the location of the huts right. Darby was never going to authorize another overnight stay in Harstad for the creosote gang to paint the correct huts.

Where else could a young man experience such diversity in life? I made a mental note about reviewing my decision to leave the Corps the following year.

DIZZY HEIGHTS

After such a good year, I continued to have second thoughts about leaving the Corps. Bill had been writing some letters to me about his experiences in the Met. It all seemed very exciting, but most of the adventures involved violent scuffles with people packing knives and high on drugs around Hackney in the East End of London. Bill also told me that he had joined the RMR (Royal Marines Reserve – London) and put in for the firearms team. Rather than make me feel like signing on for the Met, this almost put me off completely. There was Bill, who had slagged off the Corps for his last three years (and he only did four-and-a-half), almost rejoining the Corps by proxy. Still, the money in the Met was twice what I was earning, and you got to go home at the end of the shift.

It was with these conflicting thoughts that I went home for Christmas leave, with my 18-month notice period rapidly running down.

By now I had become aware that there were a number of marines who came from my home town spread around the Corps, with two from my unit, 42 Commando, and others from 40 Commando. We used to meet up on leave and thoroughly enjoy each other's company over lunchtime drinking sessions which invariably went into 'big eats sessions' at some local cafe before the drinking started properly again in the evening.

Tim from 40 Commando was heavily into 'silly rigs' runs. Tim was over 6ft tall and thinning on top, with a large nose on very masculine features. On a number of occasions, he would disappear whilst the lunchtime drinking session was in full flow and return about thirty minutes later, having visited the Oxfam shop. He would walk into the bar wearing an old lady-style blue crimplene matching skirt and jacket, and a purple hat with a large pheasant feather sticking out of the side. The thing is that he used to just do this on his own, without any prompting, and walk through the centre of the town back to the pub, having left his jeans and T-shirt on the racks in the Oxfam shop. Eventually, we got so used to his antics that we didn't even bat an eyelid when he walked back into the pub in a flowery summer dress with his size 11 desert boots sticking out of the bottom.

My brother would join in these lunchtime sessions, and would invariably bring some of his mates along from his football team. My brother was slightly older than me and had been into the pub thing for a few more years, but I was rapidly catching up. He and his mates were always up for a laugh, even if they didn't actually join in with the 'silly rigs' runs. They would stand around sometimes, looking incredulous at the transvestite dressed in a nurse's outfit who had just walked through the doors and started to chat with these tough Royal Marines without the conversation pausing and being passed the beer that he had left on the bar.

Another young marine called Buster was visiting Tim at the time and staying with his parents over Christmas leave.

Buster had stood on an anti-personnel mine whilst on a night patrol in the Falklands. He had lost his right leg from just below the knee and was now regaining his confidence with a false lower limb. He had spent some time on crutches during his recovery, but was on the mend and had only recently gotten used to walking unaided again. Buster's party piece was to take off his false leg in a bar and fill up the hollow where his stump was located with about half a pint of beer. He would then lift the leg in the air, with his size-12 trainer still attached, and knock back the beer. Of course, as the evening progressed we would all pass the false leg around and drink from the stump hollow, whilst Buster hopped around patiently awaiting his turn.

On New Year's Eve, we all decided to go along with Tim's request and go out in 'silly rigs'. Togas were always popular, but as it was New Year's Eve, we went out in tartan togas, having raided Halfords for all their tartan car blankets.

This outfit had the added bonus that in just about every pub we went into, the girls wanted to see if we were wearing anything under our kilts. I have never been groped so much in all my life. Girls would dare you to let them feel under the kilt to see if it was true, and being a bunch of tarts with very few morals, we just let them. Even Tim got lucky using this ploy, making a quick but dubious lunchtime visit to the ladies' toilets of the pub with some giggling and willing girl. This was much to the outrage of her friend, who had in the meantime gotten into a debate with one of the lads about the difference between 'Squaddies' and 'Bootnecks', she having been no doubt let down in the past by both organizations.

The evening progressed, and as was the tradition in my town, those who were still left ended up gathering around the 40ft Christmas tree in the town centre as midnight closed in. Buster was still going strong and announced that he would race anyone to the top of the tree. I immediately took him up on the challenge, and we hopped over the barriers surrounding the base of the tree and started to climb. The crowd started to roar with approval as Buster made fast progress up the tree using an arm-over-arm technique. His upper body was so strong from bearing his weight during his recovery period that I stood no chance. Still, never one to turn down an opportunity to perform for an audience, I decide to lift the tartan car blanket and flash my backside to the crowd whilst pausing halfway up. The response was encouraging; people were clapping and cheering, and I realized that I had missed my vocation in life. I should have gone on the stage.

The reaction of the crowd was intoxicating. Every time I paused and bared my backside, a huge roar erupted. Eventually, I got to the top of the tree and met Buster, who was perched right at the top of the thinnest of branches, waving at the crowd and looking mighty precarious. I was fairly hammered, but was not so shit-faced not to realize that 40ft was an awfully long way to fall, especially onto concrete. Buster had no such fears, and proved it by starting to swing the top of the tree backwards and forwards. The tree top bent, with both of us clinging on, right over the barriers below. I could see that by the way some of the crowd were moving away that we were not carrying out an approved technique as recognized by the Christmas Tree Fairies' Health and Safety Directive.

The tree swung back on the other arc, with Buster putting all his weight into the swing. I decided that it was time for a bit of self-preservation and climbed down to about 6ft from the top. Just as I was finding my footing, I heard a creaking, splintering sound and the top 6ft of the tree snapped off, leaving me looking at the splintered end of the stump and the well-lit second floor of the Town Hall at eye level.

I looked down to see Buster bouncing through the pyramid-shaped tree. As he fell through the branches, his limbs and neck got caught on the tinsel decorations and the Christmas tree lights. What must have taken hours to decorate, Buster dragged off in just a few seconds. Thankfully, the lights' cables slowed him down and prevented any nasty injury. I could tell this by the way he hit the ground, bounced up again and vaulted over the barriers before any of the approaching policemen got anywhere near him.

I cheered him on his way as he made his escape through the crowd. I then looked down, and all I could focus on was the gathering of constables at the base of the tree, none of whom had appreciated the subtle sense of humour involved in wrecking their town's Christmas tree whilst they were on duty. Some of the young policemen were salivating at the prospect of an easy 'nick' and no doubt being the first one on the scoreboard for 1984.

By this time, the previous support that I had enjoyed from the crowd had turned into a gladiatorial audience just waiting for the moment that the outnumbered but plucky Celt (me) got slaughtered and carted out of the arena by the Roman centurions (the police).

I hit the pavement running, and after feigning a few dashes at the barrier, I went for a gap. I dived head-first through the gap between two older, more rounded policemen with large red noses, did a forward roll and was up on my feet and running. I made my way through the crowd and had just gotten to a point near the edge of the gathering when a large pair of hands grabbed hold of my car blanket and hauled me towards them. It was a group of Scottish blokes who wished to congratulate me on wearing a kilt and climbing to the top of the tree. They plied my lips with a hip flask of whiskey and kept saying things like, 'You know what, that was just so funny, come and have a drunk with us', in a drunken Scottish accent.

The next pair of hands on me was wearing black leather gloves and belonged to a tall bobby built like a brick shithouse. I gave little resistance, as despite my drunken state, I still had a healthy sense of self-preservation. To the protests of the crowd, I was placed in the back of a panda car and hauled off to the local police station.

The cell block was heaving with drunks banging on cell doors, people being frog marched in wearing handcuffs, and policemen walking around looking serious, no doubt wishing that the night would end so they too could have a beer to see in the New Year quietly themselves. I was put before the custody sergeant, an older, seen-it-all, done-it-all type, maybe with grown-up children older than me. There was no point in messing about. I think I had sobered up completely by this point. These were not Naval Reggy Patrols and it would be difficult to have them over. So I just played the polite, obedient serviceman and hoped that the marked difference in my attitude, compared to the rest of the inmates shouting and screaming, would be noticed and would get me time off for good behaviour.

'What's this young man here for?' the sergeant said to the heavily built but fairly fresh-faced bobby who had arrested me. He related the story and I was pleased to see the corners of the sergeant's mouth twitch when the flashing of the backside was mentioned. Was that the start of a smile, or was it a nervous affliction from working in the cell block for too long?

I stood before him almost at attention in what remained of my Halfords car blanket.

'Well,' the sergeant said, turning to me, 'you've heard what the officer has just reported, have you anything you would like to say?'

I explained politely that I was in the Royal Marines and produced my ID card from my sock. I also apologized but did point out that the arrest for criminal damage, though understandable, was perhaps not strictly accurate as it had been the other unknown person who had dragged all the decorations off the tree. I had merely climbed up and down the tree.

'Is this correct?' the sergeant quizzed the arresting officer, who immediately turned red and started to fluff his lines by way of explanation.

'Why the fuck are we arresting people for having fun?' the sergeant bawled at the red-faced PC. 'We've got a cell block full of idiots and it's New Year's Eve! And you bring in some squaddie who's not even that pissed?'

I was about to correct the sergeant and say that I wasn't a squaddie, I was in fact a Royal Marine and was actually very pissed at the time, but decided better of this and to quit whilst I was ahead.

I was booked in and taken straight to the fingerprint room, where the large policeman started to take my prints, saying that it would speed things up if we did this now.

He seemed a conscientious, decent fellow, and I passed the time talking to him about how long he had been in the force and such like as he fingerprinted me with his huge hands, like bunches of bananas, awkwardly filling in the small boxes on the forms with ticks, crossings out and my details. I said that I hoped he wouldn't be in trouble with the sergeant, and he informed me that the sergeant always picked on the new blokes, adding that the sergeant's son was in the Army, which was probably why he had reacted like that.

Before I knew it, I was led to the side door of the police station and was outside again. The sergeant said that I would get a call or a letter telling me when I had to appear again at the station. He then went back to the queue of policemen waiting in the corridor with the latest batch of drunken people hauled in, some with blood all over their shirts and others being restrained on the floor.

I bimbled home in my tartan blanket, reflecting on what a great night it had been, but was a bit unsure as to what had happened at the police station. I had no court date, so assumed that I had just been cautioned. It was a shame that I had missed my brother and his mates, but I was sure that they would already be home. I arrived home and let myself in. The house was in darkness. I raided the fridge of some cold chicken (why is it that Mums' fridges are always full of tasty titbits?) and went to bed.

My brother turned on my bedside light and I woke up. It was 4.00 am and he had only just gotten in.

'How come you got home so quickly? I thought that you were going to spend the night in the cells?' he inquired.

I explained the story, and my brother told me that he and a mate had almost got nicked themselves because they had put up such a stink at the front desk of the police station when they had gone to demand my immediate release, only to be told by the front desk clerk that no prisoner of that name was in the cells. This was true at that time, because I had just been released out of the side door. Quite naturally, they didn't believe him and started to think of conspiracy theories. 'He's only just come back from the Falklands fighting for his country and you lock him up for nothing and then deny that he's in there?'

After some threats and a bit of banging on the desk – being careful, of course, not to actually damage anything – they were both escorted from the police station by four burly coppers, who informed them that if they carried on like they were, they would both get to see first-hand that I wasn't in their cell block. They walked home, convinced of a conspiracy.

I got up and joined my brother in another serious fridge raid. We laughed together about the events of the night. I was touched that my brother was so concerned for me that he had spent four hours at the police station, and then walked home, having missed any lift offered or taxi service.

Because he still lived at home, he was well-practised at making huge 'Scooby snack' sandwiches from the leftovers in the fridge. We grinned at each other as we tucked into the hand-sized, generously filled sandwiches in the dim light of the kitchen lamp. We had both had a close scrape but had come out smiling. Despite some brotherly fallings out as we were growing up, my brother had turned out a really good egg, and I think he was quite proud of his kid brother as well. We were happy to be in each other's company and nothing more needed to be said.

On my return to camp, I felt I had to tell my sergeant major of the events of New Year's Eve. I remembered that it could get you in even more shit if you didn't tell them that you had been arrested by the civvy police. I did this well aware that it could just be a rouse spread by RSMs and the like. How would the Corps find out anyway?

The sergeant major was quite good about it; he had only recently rejoined the Corps after spending three years in the civvy police. I had also covered the point about joining the police myself. He gave me the expected advice that maybe it would be a good idea to try in a few years' time, when I would have demonstrated that such incidents were all in the past and only a passing phase I was going through.

He gave me that world-weary 'seen it all before' look as only a copper can, or a long-in-the-tooth sergeant major; the look that made you feel really small and sober without saying a word. The sergeant major had practised this look on many defaulters, and I left his office feeling like a dejected dog having incurred the wrath of his master.

A few days later, the sergeant major accepted the withdrawal of my eighteen months' notice as if I were asking him to sign a weekend leave request. So I was signing on and staying.

I had just had my most enjoyable year in the Corps thus far, and although the age of 27 (which I would be at the end of my nine-year engagement with the Corps that I had just signed on for) seemed like a lifetime away, I was secretly pleased that I would not have to worry about finding another job. Nor would I be yomping around the streets of Hackney at 2 in the morning with a big hat and a small wooden truncheon. The unit was off on another Norway trip, followed by a six-month Northern Ireland tour. That would keep me busy; maybe a chance to save up a few pounds for that open-topped sports car I had my eye on. Then who knows? I was an old sweat of five years' service, I had a great bunch of mates, the Corps had all sorts of opportunities to offer and the world was my oyster.

YOUNG OFFICERS

Young Officers (YOs) – a.k.a. snottys or Ruperts – were mostly harmless bright young men, straight out of Uni. No doubt the cream of society, but initially hopeless at leading a troop of thirty marines. Some marines who had joined straight from school had been in five years, done two tours of Ireland, been to the Falklands and were the same age as these YOs straight out of their training. There is no doubt that the officers who the Royal Marines select are of a very high standard, and the fact that they go over the same assault courses as the non-commissioned ranks but have to be quicker gives them perhaps more respect than their army counterparts. Of course, this respect doesn't stop marines from taking advantage of the situation and testing their leaders.

Sergeants tend to give the leadership at troop level, whilst dispensing the benefit of their experience and training to the YO. If a YO is foolish enough not to take the advice from the troop sergeant, then they can make the situation worse if they don't take subtle hints such as, 'Well, Sir, we normally find that in such situations as this, if we do X, Y or Z, we tend to lose fewer men that way.'

If at this stage the YO continues with his predetermined plan, then the troop/company carry out the exact orders and makes a pig's ear of the whole situation. Comments have been placed on YOs' reports by company commanders such as, 'The men will follow this officer, if only out of interest.' It is a cruel process, but it does turn out some excellent officers. I used to think that the leadership in the Corps was poor until I left and joined the police, and then found out that the leadership of the Royal Marines is probably the best there is.

Whilst I was on the Junior Command Course (JCC) at Lympstone in 1985, in order to gain the dizzy heights of corporal, an internal security exercise was held by the YO training team in order to test their skills in riot control.

This situation was supposed to relate to circumstances similar to Northern Ireland, patrolling in a built-up area where community tensions are high; constantly being vigilant to a sniper or ambush whilst on foot patrol, when all of a sudden the patrol is surrounded by an aggressive, angry mob bent on lynching them. Further backup is then called in, in the form of riot teams with shields and riot helmets, who then successfully disperse the unruly rioters and everything calms down.

That's the plan anyway. The whole JCC was tasked to act as enemies against the YOs. Both sides relished the chance to have a go at each other – the experienced corporals who knew a trick or two about riot training and had all seen action in NI, and the keen rugby-playing young officer types who had something to prove.

In this batch of YOs was a VIP, Prince Edward. He was going through his training at the time, it being a real coup for the Corps to have a member of the royal family in their ranks. Standards were not going to be dropped, however.

There was a buzz that he was doing well in training and getting through the course. Why he left later on is a question for his conscience; it was all a bit unresolved and still is today. Why didn't he just stay for a few years and then leave? At least he could have worn a military uniform on Remembrance Day instead of bimbling around the Cenotaph in civvies, causing further embarrassment to the royal family, whilst the rest of them decided whether they were going to be a general of some other illustrious regiment for the day or a First Lord of the Admiralty, with gold rings, medals and parrots. I heard that Prince Phillip made the comment that Princess Anne should have joined the Royal Marines instead of Edward, as she, in his opinion, would have completed training and made a first-class Royal Marine officer. He was probably right, and with today's equal opportunities and her Olympic sporting talents and drive, she would be Commandant General of the Royal Marines by now.

The exercise consisted of the normal scenario: an incident occurs, the locals feel that the security forces have overreacted, and they all come out onto the streets and try to commit mass murder of some well-meaning and thoroughly decent chaps (us Royal Marines) who, after all, only wanted to help keep order and drink tea with the locals.

Anyway, in this scenario, we were the ones hurling the half bricks at the YOs' riot shields. It was too good a chance to turn down, and we entered into the spirit of the exercise with the full gusto required of such an opportunity.

Knowing that 'Eddie' was present in the unrecognizable riot-helmeted ranks of the invaders of our turf, we thought that it would be a good idea if we could kidnap him as they sent out 'snatch squads' to break up our disorderly behaviour. It was all a matter of identification.

The battle commenced. We taunted and threw bricks at the ranks of YOs, whilst they fired blank rubber bullets at us and charged us with shields and batons, never getting anywhere near us as we ran away each time. We were, of course, very fit; we were, after all, on the JCC and had all built up our fitness for the course.

The next snatch squad was sent out with a volley of blank rubber bullets to disperse the crowd. The squad charged out like an international rugby team intent on scoring a try against arch-rivals. They passed the low brickworks of the mock-up town and careered on towards the bulk of the protesters. Unbeknown to the enthusiastic YOs, they ran straight past an ambush point of the corporal's course. Four of the JCC, having thought they had identified 'Eddie', ran up behind the unsuspecting YO and nabbed him.

He was dragged off behind the low wall and the whistle was blown, indicating that it was time for the snatch squad to return. This they did, minus one prominent member.

The crowd closed in again in front of the shields to continue the riotous assembly. Meanwhile, the poor unfortunate YO was stripped off, bollocky buff, not a stitch left on him. As his riot helmet was undone, the JCC were disappointed to see that they had not bagged their main prize of Prince Edward. Still, this wriggling, white, naked YO would do. He was thrown up and down in the air by the JCC in front of the ranks of the YOs, like someone celebrating their 21st birthday in a nudist colony. The whistle blew and the DS (Directing Staff) restored order. The poor naked unfortunate collected his kit from behind the wall and, to the chant of 'Get them down, you Zulu warrior' from the whole JCC, made his way back to the ranks of YOs.

Meanwhile, the YOs back behind the riot shields laughed nervously at one of their number running towards them naked and clutching his kit. Most likely, they were thinking that they themselves might just hold back a bit and allow Edward to show true leadership on the next snatch squad charge, and let him get ahead in front next time.

We received a debrief and a smiling bollocking of approval from the DS. We hoped that the DS may be silly enough to allow us to be enemies again for the YOs on another field exercise, and we looked forward to the opportunity of seeking further royal disapproval.

HANGOVER CURE

I t had been a bad night, but as we relaxed in the swimming pool, taking light exercise and swimming up and down, the hangovers gradually abated. In a couple of hours' time, the 'mighty munches' might kick in, signifying the final end to the hangover from hell.

A small group of friends had finally got together and done the Greek package holiday routine. Very pleasant it was too for a week, with little on the itinerary other than going out, eating nice meals and having a beer. Maybe even a chance to trap off with some real girls, but in the meantime, we had the pool to relax by in the afternoons.

Trevor was obviously feeling under the weather more than most; he stood in the pool, bent forward, resting his head on his folded arms at the side of the pool. He refused to speak to anyone, only able to mutter 'Piss off' to those who tried to engage him in conversation, usually about a greasy breakfast. He then got out of the pool, purchased a large soft drink from the poolside bar, sat on the edge of the pool and stared at the drink, knowing it was the kill-or-cure remedy he needed. After he had drunk half of the fizzy concoction, he started swallowing hard and looked in the direction of the poolside toilets next to the bar, judging the time and distance it would take him to get there in a rush.

Another two sips later and he was off, running as fast as his alcohol-weary body would carry him. As he neared the louvre-swinging doors, his hand went to his mouth and he took on the look of someone blowing up a party balloon as he tried to complete his dash without yakking up on the poolside. He went to the nearest cubical, booted open the swing doors with his right foot and followed through with a lunge of his upper body as he projectile vomited in the approximate direction of the toilet.

The barman sitting on the toilet was taken by complete surprise as he was covered from head to knee with an extraordinary volume of puke. He was used to the antics of British holidaymakers in the evening getting too drunk and being ill, but having just come on duty at 10.00 am, this was too much. Trevor did his best to make amends by using a nearby towel left on a sunbed by a German holidaymaker to wipe him down as he walked around, holding his arms out as if surrendering, but he blew it when he had to quickly return to the cubical as the carrots came up again.

DEAL

I was in my last week in the Corps, finally being due to leave after eleven years. I cast my mind back to when I had signed on again, remembering that my engagement was due to finish in 1989, making me 27. I also remembered not bothering too much about this date and age because it was such an awfully long way into the future; by that stage in my life, I would be old and would surely have a clue as to what I wanted to do next.

Time had moved on, and if I decided to put pen to paper and sign on the dotted line again, it would mean serving the full twenty-two years, making me 40 when I finally left. This was too much like planning ahead and felt a bit like signing on for the same old routine until I became an old man.

I was now also in what would be called a cushy number. I was an experienced carpenter working in a large boatshed, completing all manner of jobs – bandstands, presentation pieces, fixing the small fleet of dinghies and boats that the trainee bandsmen used. There was also a good chance for some 'rabbit' work on private jobs, just to keep my skills up, you understand.

Reflecting back, I'd had quite a 'brochure life' in the Corps. I had literally been all around the world, visiting six continents, and had the bonus of sailing to many of them on adventure sailing training. I'd been involved in Northern Ireland and one of the most successful and plucky conflicts that British forces have ever been involved in, the Falklands War. I learnt a trade as a carpenter, got qualified as a skipper on yachts, learnt to ski, and the list goes on. I was lined up for the next sergeant's course or Senior Command Course (SCC), and was informed that when I passed I would be promoted straight away to 45 Commando in Arbroath and that they were lined up for a six-month tour of West Belfast next year. 'What an opportunity,' the QM said, with a genuine belief that I'd think it a good idea too. But it struck me suddenly that I did not think this was a good idea. I had been to both 45 Commando and NI, and whilst both were a good experience once, they may not be twice.

That lunchtime, I spoke to a couple of lads in the galley and told them of my dilemma. They had no sympathy and also failed to remark about what a great opportunity the sergeant's course was. One said, 'Don't drip over us. I am joining Kent Constabulary next month and he is joining HM Prison Service, and we are both taking a pay rise! Plus we get to go home every night.'

Wow! It was like a revelation. Maybe this was my chance too and I didn't have to spend all of my working life in the Corps. The Corps had been great for me, but I had seen it all and done it all, plus the Berlin Wall seemed a bit dodgy on its foundations and the USSR appeared no longer to be the threat that had motivated all Western forces for so long. Maybe it was time to change too. So I skipped over to the education officer and mentioned my – or rather my friend's – ideas. He also thought it was a good idea and handed me two sample initial exam papers for Kent, Devon and Cornwall police so that I could practice my spelling and maths.

It seemed that I only had the QM to convince. He was a super chap called Captain Gill. He was in his last few years in the Corps and had become an officer later in his career, having come up through the ranks. He was the one who encouraged me to put in for the SCC. He had also been in 45 Commando from 1966–1968 when they had deployed to Aden in a conflict that was similar to Afghanistan, with similar British casualty rates.

I had mentioned that my Dad had been a troop sergeant in 45 Commando in Aden, and he got quite excited and said that his first sergeant in 45 Commando at Aden had been a Sergeant Lewis – did I have any photos?

I asked if I could borrow some from my Mum's collection, and she lent me the best copies she had from that time: Mess dress on evenings out, side pose; black and white photos making him look like a 1950s film star. I showed these to Captain Gill the following Monday and he was excited to inform me that, 'Yes, yes, that is your Dad.'

Well, I knew this. 'But was he your first sergeant?' I inquired. 'Yes, that's what I meant,' he answered, and we were both genuinely delighted that this was the case.

The conversation carried on as he regaled a story of how, when he was a new marine and had just joined 45 Commando, my Dad was his troop sergeant. His company was out on patrol, trying to cut off some rebels who had just raided the area, causing casualties to villagers and service personnel. My Dad's troop was tasked with clearing a deeper valley with steep jebels (rocky mountain tops) on either side. Apparently, my Dad had decided, sensibly, to send up recce patrols on each side of the valley rather than march straight down the valley into a probable ambush. Up went Marine Gill and his section on the left flank. As they neared the top of the jebel, they were opened up on from above with a few machine guns that had been lying in wait for the company to move down through the valley, which would have caused untold losses. As Marine Gill saw and felt his first action, the section halfway up the other side of the valley opened up on the machine gunners and put them to flight, killing or wounding several of them. The company then pressed on unmolested and succeeded in their task.

Captain Gill said that it was a truly inspiring action, and although my Dad had got him shot at for the first time, he and the others considered it a significant lifesaving decision to send the recce patrols up first.

Finally on the cusp of leaving the Corps, I had found a serving member of the Corps who had served with my Dad and had told me a great titbit about him in Aden. My burning desire to find out what my Dad had experienced in the Corps was finally fading; I had discovered what he had been through, and I had all the memories, mates, photos and short clips of ITN news to prove it.

So I had to inform the boss who knew my Dad, who had put me in for the SCC, that I wanted to leave and join the police. The following week, I knocked on his door and informed him of my decision.

'Well, why not?' he said. 'You are a young man still and the police is a great career. I would have done it a few years ago myself, but I think I am too old now.' He was so supportive.

The RSM made similar comments about trying something else before you get too old and that there was a big wide world out there.

It was, with mixed feelings that I started my leaving routine at Deal. A small town on Kent's Channel coast, Deal is where the Royal Marines School of Music was based. It was one of the few places that I served where the locals fully integrated with the marines, and vice versa.

During the summer, the atmosphere was almost Victorian when outdoor concerts were held on the lawns of the barracks. Half of the local population would attend, lay out their picnic blankets and set up to listen to the orchestra. They would play a range of music, from classical to up-tempo versions of more modern classics and themes from films and television, showing off the varied talent of the orchestra. Bottles of wine were opened as the sun sank on the warm and balmy evenings that always finished with the bugles and trumpets playing a perfect rendition of 'Sunset'. The atmosphere was truly unique.

There were many elderly people in the audience, but many of the same young faces that were seen in popular local pubs were also there in groups seated on the lawn; they had grown up in Deal and this was just part of the town's summer they had known all their lives. Many of these concerts were held throughout the year for various charities, for the development of the junior band and the sheer pleasure of playing music.

The 'leaving routine' is a legendary time in a service person's life. It is used by many old hands as an excuse to loaf off for the best part of their last six months, and can be the ultimate excuse should they be given a job that they would wish to avoid, saying, 'Sorry, sergeant major, but I am on my leaving routine.' On the other hand, the sergeant major could be finally getting rid of a marine who is a right pain in the arse!

'I'm on my leaving routine Sarge,' would be the slovenly reply to any order detailing a leaver for some arduous task as they bimbled off to the NAAFI for a cup of tea and a sticky bun. What with vocational training courses to attend, kit to track down (or proff, if it's been misplaced) and hand in, and of course various piss-ups to attend, the life of a Royal Marine on a leaving routine could be quite hectic.

I attended the records office three months before my leaving date, expecting to be given my leaving routine card and therefore my ticket to bimbling around camp and eating vast quantities of sticky buns for a few weeks. Mitch, the records Wren, viewed my leave card, made a few quick calculations and stated that with my one month's terminal leave added to my owed summer leave, I could leave next week if I wished and still have two-and-a-half months off on full pay.

I was slightly taken aback. Not only did this mean that I was actually going to take my uniform off and leave the cosseted world of the Royal Marines within a few days, but I was also going to have to complete the world's quickest leaving routine. Mitch and I set the date for my leaving there and then, and I marched off clutching my leaving record on a mission to complete three months loafing around in a few days.

Two devastating events then happened in my life, and that of my family.

Just after leaving the Corps, my brother, Stephen, was taken ill and seemed to be going downhill. He was taken to the hospital in severe pain in early August, and the specialists diagnosed the late stages of cancer that can strike younger men. His white blood cell count was very low, indicating that it was at an advanced stage, and on a further scan they informed us and his young wife that he only had about two weeks to live. I spent the next six weeks trying to deal with his unexpected death and support my lovely Mum and supportive wife, whom I had married whilst at Deal just the year before, as well as Sally, Stephen's young widow. We were all rocked, but I met many of Stephen's super friendship group and they could not do enough for us.

The following month, five weeks after my brother's death on 11 August 1989, I joined the police. I was with a good bunch on my intake of twelve other trainees. The two trainers were also very helpful, obviously experienced constables. I sat there on my first morning in black police trousers, a crisp white shirt and a black tie, with shoes polished up to RM standard. I must admit I was healthily nervous, as I had just turned down an almost certain pass and promotion to be a sergeant in the Royal Marines. If I found the police training difficult, or I failed the course, I would be unemployed. Jerry and Derek, our trainers, put us at ease. When questions were asked, they used the technique of bouncing it back to the class, saying, 'What do you think?' Then someone in the class would give the answer. This carried on all morning during the introductions. It wasn't what I had expected and came as quite a pleasant surprise.

In the afternoon, I asked, 'So, is this how police training goes? We ask a question, you bounce it back and rely on someone to know the answer already in the group, as just under the surface we all know most of this stuff as it's common sense?' Jerry turned to Derek, and they nodded and said, 'A good observation, but you need to know this law book too.' They held up the hefty police guidance manual. It was a thick book and probably not the best read ever, but I sat up in my chair feeling that I had made the right decision.

Here I was, at the turn of the autumn in a centrally heated room with nice, well-motivated people. I was wearing a nice new shirt and tie and had very little responsibility, other than joining in and learning a large book. I have a very interesting career ahead of me, I thought. That month, if I had stayed in the Royal Marines, I would have deployed with 45 Commando to West Belfast as a Sergeant RM, maybe in charge of a troop of thirty marines and a young officer for six months. I was also taking a 4K pay rise from Corporal Lewis RM to PC Lewis.

On 22 September, during the first week of police training, I was watching the morning news at police headquarters before going down to the classroom to start the day's lessons. The aerial pictures taken from a news helicopter that was being broadcast live were of a flat-roofed building destroyed by a bomb blast. As the helicopter flew over the site, I recognized my friend's white-painted house just in front of the demolished building, and realized that Deal Barracks had just been bombed by the IRA.

Eleven young men with everything to live for had been murdered, and many more had been seriously injured. I was a powerless observer. I could not help move rubble or provide first aid. I could, though, provide support. When the time was right, I made a few phone calls and attended several funerals, but felt like an outsider as I saw the faces of my friends carrying coffins and standing in small insular groups in obvious shock. I have never heard a violin played to such perfection and passion as when the most talented of the Royal Marines School of Music played laments for their friends and colleagues in wooden boxes covered in the Union Flag at the front of the church. As 'Adagio for Strings' filled every corner of the church, many allowed themselves to openly weep.

The band marched through Deal a few days later with eleven gaps in their ranks, and the whole population turned out to respectfully clap and cheer them as they went past, playing with tears rolling down their cheeks but without missing a note. An officer summed up the feeling of that parade when he said, 'It's sticking two fingers up to the IRA.'

I don't think Deal ever recovered from this attack. A twelve-sided bandstand was constructed on the seafront, and on eleven of the sides, the name of each musician who lost his life was carved. A few short years later, defence cuts saw Deal Barracks close down and be turned into flats and housing. The Royal Marines School of Music moved to Portsmouth, leaving no one to regularly play in the bandstand.

I visited Deal again recently. The town is expanding and traffic has become heavier, but the barracks are just about recognizable. Behind the preserved and listed facades of buildings, people go about their business, feeling smug that house prices are on the rise again in the south-east. If not the heart, then the soul had been ripped out of Deal. It's now just another growing and prosperous south-coast town. Many of the now ageing local population must still hark back to those halcyon days of the summers of the 1970s and 1980s, when the bugles of the Royal Marines School of Music played as the sun set over picnic blanket-strewn playing fields.

I had left the Corps, yet I found myself grieving silently and guiltily without my support network. What right did I have to feel that I was a victim when I had not even been there? Just as I thought I had left behind the experience of regularly losing friends to violence at a surprisingly high peacetime attrition rate, I had dropped my guard and suffered as a result, for months if not years. But that was only a fraction of the suffering of those whose families lost a loved one or one of the many young bandsmen who were disabled for life.

Life went on, and I followed the investigation. It would seem that changing the guard at the barracks from regular Royal Marines to a private security firm had tipped the balance. When a small IRA active service unit moved into a holiday let in a nearby street, they only had to step over a low fence and plant their device in the band's rest room, then set it for the time they had observed the band arriving for work. There was no great risk to the IRA team. It was a soft target, made softer by defence cuts and employing people more suited to looking after industrial estates.

The police investigation was able to trace the house that the active service unit used to recce and walk from to plant the bomb. A taxi driver was also found who had picked up or dropped someone off at the house, but the investigation seemed to draw a blank. No doubt today's forensics methods would have obtained DNA and other evidence, but even if this had been available and the terrorists had been convicted, the Good Friday Agreement implemented a few years later would have seen them released in the late 1990s.

TENUOUS LINKS TO GLORY

In 2010, my son and I drove down to Portsmouth so that he could attend an interview for a job as a sailing instructor on a beach in the Mediterranean. We stayed at a hotel in Portsmouth, and on the day of the interview, I was going to have about four or five hours to kill.

I thought that this would be a good opportunity to visit the Royal Marines Museum in the old Eastney Barracks. I had visited it once in training, but that was a long time ago and more history had been made since then.

As it was a weekday, I was one of only about four people visiting, so I had lots of time to read about the exhibits. I would not be boring any of my family, who quite often feigned interest when I slowly walked around a historic building or display such as this.

Straight away, I started to recognize some of the exhibits on display outside the museum. Various landing craft that I had actually been on were now statues commemorating the era in which I had served. This felt odd, as I'd thought I was going to see an awful lot about Nelson and the Second World War. They also had an even more recent Afghanistan display, which I was certainly interested in.

I made my way around the museum, fascinated at the tangible items on display and their link to RM and British history.

I then came upon a display cabinet that had the red uniform jacket worn by Marine Sergeant Secker, who caught Nelson as he fell at Trafalgar. There it was, even with some dark-coloured dry blood on the sleeve. This was serious stuff! I had recently seen the actual bullet that killed Nelson on display in a cabinet at Windsor Castle.

The next display cabinet had the sword worn and used by Captain Bamford VC during the raid on Zeebrugge in 1918. I had heard about him too in Corps history lessons during training. He was a real legend in the Corps, one of the holders of the Victoria Cross for his action at Zeebrugge.

In the very next cabinet display was the 84mm anti-tank weapon fired at the Argentine corvette ARA *Guerrico* by the Royal Marines defending South Georgia in April 1982. Wow! I knew the bloke who actually fired that, I mused to myself.

It was a class action by the small detachment of Royal Marines who had been landed on the island by the Royal Navy ice patrol ship HMS *Endurance* at the start of the campaign in order to expel some illegal Argentine scrap metal workers who were backed by the Argentine military. They were also briefed to defend the island, but to only 'make a token resistance' so as to cause the Argentinians to use force so that there was no question that it was an unprovoked armed aggression. Lieutenant Mills, the young officer in charge of the RM detachment, read the signal and replied, 'Sod that, we will make their eyes water.'

The detachment of twenty-two marines then dug in on a hillside overlooking King Edward Cove and waited to hand out some 'token resistance'. They were all armed to the teeth with whatever guns and ammo they had found stored in the bowels of HMS *Endurance*.

Several of my friends had deployed to the Falklands that year as part of the peacetime NP 8901 detachment of the Falklands and the ship's detachment of HMS *Endurance*. Just about all of them later joined 42 Commando and J Company in the Falklands, once they had been captured, released and returned home, then volunteered to return as part of 42 Commando. My friend Jock Hunter, when I met up with him on the *Canberra* on the way down south, told me how he and his fellow marines had so much ammo that they were standing on full boxes of 7.62mm GPMG ammo. They had put up some serious resistance and gave a good account of themselves. We, who had not yet fired a shot in this conflict, could only listen to their stories, holding them in semi-hero status as they had actually 'been there and done that'. Jock described the action with the phrase, 'It was Wazza!'

The first the marines knew that the island was being assaulted was when an Argentine Alouette helicopter was seen flying over the Grytviken settlement. Another Puma helicopter was seen to drop troops off out of sight and out of the line of fire from their positions, but close enough to be a serious threat. When the Puma returned with more reinforcements, the pilot flew too close to the Royal Marines' position, and it was shot down in a hail of intense machine-gun and small- arms fire. There were several casualties and the helicopter ended up crashing into the hillside opposite.

'Well, that's given them something to think about,' the sergeant of the detachment had announced.

Next, the Argentinian corvette made an appearance and sailed into King Edward Cove. The frigate-sized ship, bristling with large-calibre naval guns and Exocet missiles, opened fire on the Royal Marine positions as it steamed past. However, the 20mm gun jammed after one shot, the 40mm gun jammed after six shots and the 100mm main gun failed to function after one shot. One can imagine the flapping that must have happened on the bridge when they realized that they had to proceed forward into the cove, then turn around and head out again, past the marines' position, with no weapon systems working other than some signal flares.

Lieutenant Mills and his team opened up with all they had from about 550 metres away, hitting the ship with hundreds of rounds. One marine fired the 84mm anti-tank gun, aiming at the bridge, but due to not having had the chance to zero his weapon, and the ship being at more than the maximum range, it hit the water about 8ft from the ship's side, then acted like a torpedo and put a hole in the vessel under the waterline. With its tail between its legs, ARA *Guerrico* sharply headed out to sea to lick its wounds and hopefully not sink.

The marines, in the meantime, continued to pour down fire on the first Argentine landing party, keeping them pinned down so they were unable to move forwards or backwards. Other Argentine marines were meanwhile landed out of range of the defending force by the Alouette helicopter, as this David and Goliath battle was in full swing in King Edward Cove.

Meanwhile, out at sea, the *Guerrico* had managed to get its main armament working again and started to fire on the Royal Marine positions.

This finally convinced Lieutenant Mills that things were over, and he ordered his marines to cease fire. He then stood on the parapet of his trench, in full view of enemy fire, and in complete disregard for his own safety he waved a white coat and surrendered his detachment. The smoking ship out at sea, the crashed helicopter on the hillside opposite and the numerous dead and wounded Argentinians around his position indicated that he had fulfilled his duty and there was no need for unnecessary further loss of life on either side.

Honourably, the Argentinian marines accepted the surrender immediately and ceased fire too.

The ARA *Guerrico* had over 50 per cent of its weapon systems put out as a result of this action, and had to return to Argentina for several weeks for repairs.

The Royal Marines were treated well by the Argentine marines whom they had surrendered to, and were quickly taken to Argentina and repatriated home via Montevideo in Uruguay. Perhaps the right-wing military dictatorship of Argentina hoped that Britain would then abandon the British citizens of the Falkland Islands to their fate. Why hold onto those British soldiers when you could prevent any further diplomatic problems by flying them straight home? How wrong they were!

So there I was in the Corps museum, viewing the 84mm weapon that had been fired from that peninsula in South Georgia. I had also, later, actually served with the combatants who had been there.

This is my historic if tenuous link to Nelson. It is a story I will tell anyone who is still listening, as I 'spin dits' gathered around a table in some bar, with a few empty pint glasses building up around us.

REUNION

I threw myself into my new career in the police force and carried on putting in for every new course I could, trying out different departments and teams. Then came a new house, a dog and two years of training, studying for an early pass at the sergeant's exam. What little time we had left in our lives was then fully absorbed by the source of my greatest joy ever, my family and children.

Carol and I didn't set out to have children, but nature played that trick on us. When you are first together, you think that the initial few years are going to last forever, but that is completely changed and enhanced by children. In our case, three of them!

I would still find myself watching something about the Royal Marines if it was on TV and I would tell the odd 'dit' at work, given the right moment, but I effectively lost contact with many oppos from the marines. As I was 300 miles away from any main RM base, I had no reason to drop in whilst passing by because I was never 'passing by'.

As the twenty-fifth anniversary of the Falklands War was coming up, I knew there would be some form of reunion. I looked it up on Google, and there was one of the lads organizing something at Bickleigh Barracks. To add to his credibility, Bungy, the ex-member of K Coy, was actually still serving and was now a major, so had a bit of clout to get such things organized. He and his small team were quick to reply and send me an invite. He also arranged for those who were up for it to attend Commando Training Centre Royal Marines first on the way to Plymouth, and the PTIs would take us around the endurance course.

I asked Mark if he wanted to come too, and he said he would. Fortunately, he had got rid of his old Avenger by this time, so it looked like we would actually get there without having to be towed by a breakdown vehicle.

Mark and I set off very early one morning in June 2007 to drive the 260 miles to CTCRM with our running kit, shower kit, smart suits and medals. We arrived in good time at CTCRM and parked up to see several other blokes who all looked vaguely familiar, but some had grey hair and some no hair at all. They all still looked pretty fit though.

What followed was a most surreal experience. I just kept meeting people who, in different circumstances, you would go for a beer with, spend hours catching up with and then arrange another meet-up. But we all spent just five minutes chatting before having someone else shake our hand or call out, 'Lew, how are you doing?'

Unlike the last time we did this, we got a lift to the start of the endurance course and the PTIs were not only friendly, they were also super-respectful and were obviously enjoying the company of these 40 to 75-year-olds doing the endurance course again.

The brief started with a bit of an embarrassed apology:

'Hi, lads. Welcome to CTC and the endurance course. As you can see, it is a very hot and sunny day today and it is so warm that Health and Safety would normally mean that if you were all in training now, we would not do the endurance course today. It is too hot and the potential for heat exhaustion is too great. I know you all did this in any weather when you were in training, and the Corps do deploy to Afghanistan and Iraq, where it is also hot, but they are the rules.'

He let this sink in for a few seconds to let the laughing stop, then added, 'However, I and a few PTIs are going for a run today around Woodberry Common. If you, as civilians, wish to follow us, it is a public common, we can't stop you, and we would enjoy your company.'

So off we went, around the obstacles and tunnels of the endurance course. We did the water tunnel, and all watched those who wanted to go through get dunked and then move on to the next feature. It was actually fun without all the equipment and rifle and having to keep running as fast as you could.

More oppos met up. Some bought sons and daughters, who also went through the various tunnels and ponds. We then reached the transport again and were given the option of a small-speed march back to CTCRM. Some even ran all the way back.

We lined up on Heart Break Lane, in three ranks, did a right turn and the PTIs commanded, 'Falkland veterans, quick march', followed by, 'Break into double time, double march.' It was a spiritual experience running with the best part of fifty or so 42 Commando Falklands Island veterans along this well-trodden lane.

Lads who were in training and working out on a nearby field had their PTIs stop their session, and they lined the hedgerows and clapped and cheered us along. It was almost a shame to stop when we got to the finish. But we had been promised a nice lunch and a beer in the sergeants' mess, so after showering we changed into our best suits, with berets and medals, just like we had seen the old blokes do when we were young.

We were provided with an excellent lunch, and because I was driving, I saved my alcohol intake for later in the day. Mark met up with some L Coy friends and had a few beers. We were then invited to have a walk around camp and look at some of the areas where we had our old accommodation blocks and the assault courses. It was whilst we were having a look at the regain ropes that some lads who had just finished their Kings Squad pass-out shouted to us from the balcony, 'Are you Falklands vets?'

We replied that we were, and one of the King's Squad said, 'What's he doing?'

We looked in the direction of the rope ladders leading to the regain ropes over the large static tank pool, and there was Mark climbing up the ropes, still wearing his beret, smart suit and polished shoes.

'I reckon I can still do a full regain,' Mark stated confidently.

Smudge and I, who were watching, just said, 'Oh my God, what is he like?', and started cracking up laughing.

More of the recently qualified Marines appeared on the balcony and started to shout encouragement as Mark swung his legs down, starting the regain manoeuvre, which if successful brings you back onto the top of the rope again like a cat crawl.

Mark swung once; Mark swung twice. He then slowed down and stopped swinging.

'He's wrapped,' the group on the balcony said as they skedaddled, as there was no way they were going to be witness to this trespass on the PTI's hallowed regain ropes.

Mark hung in mid-air, unable to climb up or go hand-over-hand to the end of the ropes.

He looked down at the cloudy cold water and dropped down, ensuring he did a decent back splat on the way in. Smudge and I rolled around laughing with tears in our eyes, and could only just help Mark out of the pool.

A short while later, we walked back into the sergeants' mess, with Mark squelching behind. We were met by the RSM, who saw the state of Mark and said in that practised menacing tone, 'Ah, so you're the clown who went for a swim then.'

Even though Mark had not been under military law for over twenty-four years, he still looked extremely uncomfortable and most likely thought he was going to spend the afternoon in the grease pit doing the washing up.

The RSM deescalated the situation when he said, 'Well, I suppose I should buy you all a pint then.' And off Mark squelched to the sergeant's mess bar to continue his reunion afternoon.

BACK TO BICKERS

We then made our way to Plymouth, and to Nigel's house. Nigel had been a Royal Marine during that time in the 1980s too, but had been shot whilst on a tour in Northern Ireland and had taken several years to recover from his wounds, so he missed the Falklands. Unfortunately, he suffered a further injury in a car accident which left him in a wheelchair with only partial mobility. He had carers looking after him in a comfortable bungalow in Plymouth, and invited Mark, Woody and myself to stay for the weekend.

We all met up and went out for a fairly low-key night before the reunion in Plymouth, and bumped into many of the lads on the reunion who had also taken the whole weekend off. I was thrilled to meet up with Joe, Bill and Neil again, and spent most of the evening talking with them.

We also got talking to one of the lads who was still serving as an RSM, who when he found out about Nigel's situation, offered to give us all a lift up to Bickleigh Barracks the following morning. That was decent of him, and we all piled in the Transit van with Nigel the following morning right on time.

I had been speaking with our newfound best mate and RSM, and it turned out he was in K Coy in the Falklands but was now RSM of the SBS. I did remember him. There were 250 turning up at this reunion, plus family members, so it was quite a turnout.

What a great Corps I had been a part of. Here was yet another example of someone we hardly knew offering his time to give us a lift, and as ever, he was so down to earth and more interested in what we had done since leaving the Corps than telling us tales of his twenty-eight years in the Corps and SBS career.

Woody volunteered to look after Nigel all day, and later said he spent most of it having people ignore him and talk to Nigel in the wheelchair, assuming that his disability was due to the Falklands. When a former or serving major general engages you and asks polite questions about how you got your injury, and you explain it was a gunshot wound, why correct them that it actually happened in Northern Ireland and not on Mount Harriet? It was a genuine 'wounded in action' after all, so why not accept all the special treatment for once and have all the senior officers queueing up to talk with you? You get to march past, in the front-rank parade, and get a good view!

Prior to the parade, we were welcomed at 42 Commando's sergeants' mess. We walked into this hallowed mess and looked at all the trophies on the wall, stemming back to the Second World War and just about every British military campaign since. There was hardly a space left, and it is a big building and bar area.

I met up with Bill, Joe and Neil again and was quickly handed a pint from somewhere. We then noticed one of our former sergeants, Frank. I had last seen him when he was an instructor or DS on the Junior Command Course. He was the most professional of soldiers, with early promotion, several tours of Ireland on various teams and sniper-trained. Always wanting to be a 'Grav' and on the front line, he had stayed in for twenty-two years and ended up a WO2. In the Falklands, he had finally got his ultimate youthful wish, leading a troop of K Coy in the historic battalion attack against well-prepared and dug-in positions. The last time the British armed forces had been involved in a conflict of that scale was in Korea in the 1950s. After the Falklands, Frank joined us in the QM's department whilst recovering from a head wound.

Frank was dressed smartly and flamboyantly in a pinstriped suit, frilly shirt and pink tie, and beckoned us over when he saw us. He was always fun and could always 'spin a good dit', and after some time catching up, we unsurprisingly turned the conversation to the Falklands, with Neil asking, 'What did happen to you on Mount Harriet? You never did tell us the story.'

Frank took a deep breath and looked like he was considering his audience and surroundings. I think he was contemplating that if you are going to tell such a personal story, then the situation has to be right, and 42 Commando's sergeants' mess surrounded by your oppos was going to be hard to beat.

'Didn't you know about my casevac?' Frank began.

He was the troop sergeant of one of the three troops of K Coy who had been tasked to go around the side of the Mount Harriet feature, under cover of darkness. Their briefing was then to make a silent approach until the enemy was alerted. All hell would be let loose on the Argentine positions by naval guns and artillery, plus mortars, and then K Coy was to move through, engage with the enemy and take the bulk of the Mount Harriet position.

As Frank was leading his troop up the mountain on the silent approach, the lead troop was getting closer and closer to the Argentine positions undetected. Fire missions were cancelled as lines drawn on a map were crossed. Then all hell indeed broke loose, and when they were within only a few hundred metres of the enemy position, K Coy was fired upon with machine-gun and rifle fire. Prearranged Argentine artillery then opened up on the assaulting commandos, who were by this time even closer to the Argentine position. It is a classic tactic of infantry to get so close to the enemy that their artillery and mortars can't engage, as they would almost certainly hit their own side, but this of course works both ways.

On K Coy went, with many dynamic and heroic individual and team actions, which kept the battle moving in favour of the attacking side.

Frank told us that quite early on in the night battle, his troops were hit by artillery fire and he received a wound in the back of his head. He said he remained conscious but could feel a large fragment of shrapnel embedded in the back of his head. One of his troop corporals called a medic and then took over as troop sergeant, leaving Frank behind as they carried on, bayonets fixed and throwing hand grenades as they closed with the enemy.

Frank made his way to the bottom of the mountain, where the medics were able to provide triage and life-saving first aid on the steady stream of wounded Royal Marines and Argentinian soldiers appearing out of the darkness from the slope of the mountain, whilst the night battle raged on amongst the craggy peaks.

Amazingly, the small evacuation Gazelle and Scout helicopters were landing at the base of the mountain under full view of enemy artillery spotters. They were landing and picking up as many wounded as possible, and ferrying them to the Brigade Maintenance Area Field Hospital or the hospital ships waiting offshore.

Frank said that the Naval Commando Medic told him that he was first on the helicopter, as he had a head wound. Frank, still fully kitted up at this time, said he was expecting to get a bandage put on his head and then go and rejoin his troop.

'No, Frank, you have a serious head wound. Get on the helicopter,' the medic commanded him.

'But what about him? He's worse than me. He has got an arm missing, and he's got bullet wounds in his leg!' Frank rebelled and tried to find an excuse to stay with his troop.

'Frank you have a hole in your head and you will go mad if you don't get to the hospital, so just get on the helicopter and leave your rifle behind!'

Frank got on the helicopter, still holding his rifle. He said he then sat in the back and watched as the two pilots calmly waited for everyone to be settled and secure on board, then casually had a conversation about which ship they could land on later that still had some good draught beer available.

Frank saw an artillery round land about 100 metres away to the right, then another an equal distance to the left. They were being bracketed, and the next round would most likely land on top of them. Frank tapped the pilot on the shoulder and made desperate lift-off motions. The pilot gave him a smile and a thumbs-up, and Frank said that it felt like the helicopter flew back down the valley at night at the slowest speed possible, avoiding rocks and nearby mountains, with shell bursts following behind them.

Frank was surprised to land on a hospital ship and was helped off the chopper by a medical orderly. Upon seeing that Frank still had his rifle with him, and at the high port, the orderly took hold of it and said, 'I will take that off you.'

Frank resisted, and he said they had a tug of war, with both sets of hands on the stock of the rifle, pulling it to and fro. The medic informed Frank that he shouldn't have brought his rifle on board in the first place, as they were a hospital ship and subject to the Geneva Convention. To have weapons on board could thus compromise their status. Frank relented and let go, and watched aghast as the orderly walked to the edge of the flight deck and threw the rifle overboard into the dark ocean below. It was only at this time that he accepted that he was in fact a casualty, and allowed himself to be taken into the operating theatre as a priority.

They quickly got him in first due to his head wound and lay him on the operating table. He had his jacket removed, and his trousers and favourite boots were cut off with scissors so that the medical team could examine his body to check he had no other shrapnel or bullet wounds. Frank said he literally had a live hand grenade fall out of a pocket and land on the operating table, only to be casually scooped up and follow the rifle into the sea.

The surgeon then turned his attention to the bleeding at the back of his head. All resuscitation, blood, fluids and crash teams were around the operating table, standing by. The surgeon reported to the team that he could see a large fragment of metal embedded in Frank's head and that, if removed, it could cause further trauma. He gently nudged the jagged lump of steel, which promptly fell onto the operating table with a metallic 'clunk'. Frank informed us that he thought his brain had fallen out, while the medical team's eyes opened wide behind their face masks as they witnessed the event.

No serious bleeding occurred and Frank stayed conscious but stunned.

'Well, I think you had a lucky escape,' the surgeon informed Frank. 'The wound is not too deep and may not have caused a brain injury, but it is difficult to tell at this stage.'

After being monitored for a few days and getting sewn up, Frank was able to assist as an orderly for many of the other patients on board with more serious injuries. Frank read and wrote letters for those with hand and eye injuries, also fetching bedpans and feeding and shaving his comrades as best as he could.

We stood in 42 Commando's sergeants' mess in silence, listening to the 'dit' of events twenty-five years ago. We refuelled our now empty pint glasses and continued to listen to Frank's story.

He informed us that the two British hospital ships were allocated a square couple of miles of sea space just off the Falkland Islands, where they steamed together with an Argentinian hospital ship. They constantly transmitted their position to all forces to prevent any attack on the ships.

At quieter times, one of the ships would steam to neutral Uruguay and unload the wounded to be repatriated to the UK or Argentina.

They would then rejoin the 2-mile square of ocean and take all incoming wounded from either side, treating them with the same priority.

This was just one revelation amongst many told that weekend. I remember looking around the room and knowing just about all of the 250 marines gathered. By name, by face, after a short while talking with them or by just swapping events of our time in the Corps and having my memory nudged.

Also there were some currently serving Royal Marines from L Coy, who had just returned from a serious tour of Afghanistan. They had received more casualties during their six-month tour than we had in the six-week Falklands campaign. I sat down with some of them for lunch, and after introducing myself the twenty-five-year age gap was closed instantly. We were all Royal Marines joining in a beer and lunch at Bickers. They told me of what daring do they got up to on their recent tour, and I tried my best to keep up with some decent 'dits' and pointed out some of the guys who were legendary figures in the Corps for their achievements. I could have been sitting with my mates in the galley of old. In fact, I was. L Coy had volunteered to return from their leave two weeks early to help out the Falklands vets and show us around. It was quite touching and they put on a great show.

The parade went off without a hitch. The poor drill Colour Sergeant did his best to remind us how to turn left and march again in three ranks. 'He's making it up as he goes along,' came the Monty Python-esque call from the rear rank as the Colour Sergeant pretended to throw his pace stick into the hedges, laughing out loud. Again, it was a spiritual moment as the Royal Marines band burst into 'Life on the Ocean Wave', the official march of the Royal Marines, while we smartly stepped out in medals and green berets as proud as any King's Squad.

THE CORPS IS 350

On the special Corps birthday of 350 years, CTCRM Lympstone put on a special event for Royal Marines Association members. There seemed to be about 500 old veterans on the parade ground that day, who had served in conflicts ranging from the Second World War to Korea, Northern Ireland, the Falklands, Iraq and Afghanistan.

The usual stances and unarmed combat displays went on, and some gathered in the galley for coffee and sandwiches.

Bob had encouraged me to attend and I was pleased to be there. We had a super day. Bob and I had a few beers later in the evening at the bar, but no chili!

Major Cameron March (still serving at that time), who had been L Coy's sergeant major in the Falklands, gave an insightful view on how the Corps was now trying to deal with mental health issues based on TRIM (Trauma Risk Management). This is a means of identifying serving military personnel with persistent mental health issues brought on by their exposure to combat or other military training situations. It also allows non-healthcare-trained personnel to monitor and manage colleagues.

My wife, Carol, and I took a quiet moment to walk around the assault course and bottom field, mainly to look at the wonderful views of the River Exe, but also so I could show off the 30ft ropes and tell her how quickly I used to climb them! Whilst we were walking up beside the gym, we saw an old veteran in a mobility scooter stuck on the slight hill.

I said to the gentleman, 'Has your battery run out? You shouldn't have done the second lap of the assault course.'

'Ah. Hello chum,' he replied. 'Yes, it has and my two mates have buggered off to the NAFFI for a beer and left me. They are also in electric buggies but have more power left.'

'Shall I give you a push up the hill?' I asked, and started to push him up the hill. I asked him from what era he had served in, and he told Carol and I that he was called Colin and was an ex-National Serviceman who had landed at Port Said, Egypt. He and his helicopter stick of Royal Marines from 45 Commando had then been shot up by friendly fire from an RAF jet that had strafed the runway. Some had been killed, the CO had his arm removed by the cannon fire and Colin had lost a leg. He pulled up his trouser leg to show us his prosthetic limb.

He told us that he had never figured out why a British RAF pilot would have shot at British helicopters, because it had been the first-ever heliborne assault in history and the Egyptians didn't have any helicopters. 'You would have thought they would have told him that before they took off,' he reflected.

I let him finish and then informed him that my Dad was also on that helicopter assault, but in a different chopper. He had seen the 'Blue on Blue' contact, but he and his stick were unharmed. Well, this of course made us best buddies as I continued to huff and puff between 'dits' as I looked forward to the slight downhill slope near the accommodation blocks, where his car and charging point were parked about 500 metres away. Where was Corporal Devaney, the one who had heaved me over the 6ft wall all those years ago during training, when you needed him?

We chatted away for a while and I left this 82-year-old veteran plugged into his car, with him promising to buy me a pint later.

The parade was fun too. Most parades are a pain, but veterans' parades are just full of old Royal Marines chatting to each other and vaguely listening to commands of 'quick march' and 'right turn', normally missing every other command because of some interesting conversation or everybody laughing too much and no one can hear the Drill Sergeant.

I was standing next to Scouse, who had been in HQ in the Falklands too. Scouse was quite a short chap, but he was also one of those people who had remained fit and slim and looked at least ten years younger than his true age. Behind us was an actual D-Day veteran from 45 Commando. He was standing unassisted but told us he couldn't hear very well and might seize up when we finally marched off, so asked us to just march around him if he was struggling.

'You can keep up Royal, we will help you,' a fellow veteran said supportively, who was sporting a serious row of six or seven medals from the Iraq conflict onwards pinned to his chest.

So the parade progressed and the current major general made the inspection of all the ranks in our company. I could hear he was enjoying himself speaking with these veterans, who represented all conflicts from 1945 to the present day. The RSM spoke with some in the ranks whom he recognized from his younger days in the Corps.

As the major general approached Scouse, he took one look at his South Atlantic Falkland medal and commented, 'My, you don't look old enough to have been involved in The Falklands.'

'To be honest, Sir, you don't look old enough to be a major general,' came the quick reply, and all around chuckled away, including the major general.

As the inspection came to an end, the RSM commanded the parade to 'Right turn, quick march'.

As we stepped off, the majority with their left foot, the D-Day veteran let go the most tremendous fart, which was audible about six ranks away. 'Oh, sorry boys. I hope you can you march around that smell too.'

The parade gradually came into step to the beat of the Royal Marines Band, and by the time they had completed one lap of the parade ground the years had dropped away and the smartest 'eyes right' ever was performed by the Green Bereted ranks, shinning medals chinking and reflecting in the bright sunshine.

THE BICKLEIGH CLOUD MAKES A GUEST APPEARANCE

Having met up again with Bill, Neil and Joe, we decided that this reunion lark was so much fun that we should meet up much more often than the twenty-odd years between when we all went our separate ways and the twenty-fifth anniversary Falklands reunion. So we formulated a plan that would see us get together every year at each other's houses and rotate this around the five-year main Bickleigh reunion. Over the years, we have enjoyed a variety of simple weekend get-togethers in rural Dorset and Suffolk, then the bright lights of London and Oxford.

We of course all meet up every five years at Bickleigh Barracks, and also had the fortieth anniversary of the Falklands campaign in 2022.

We all get a lot out of these meet-ups and they remain popular, with the numbers ever increasing as we are now joined by some quite grown-up grandchildren of veterans in addition to the wider family and friends viewing from the stands set up on the parade ground. 42 Commando's Falklands reunion embraces all those 'Ex Booties' who find themselves too far from Arbroath and 45 Commando's reunion, or maybe they were on a ship's detachment 'Down South' and want to feel part of it again. I notice Bungy and his team have put in much effort to make them all feel welcome.

Amongst the favourite old tales told time and again at bars around the Corps, occasionally a new gem will emerge from some greying veteran who has hidden it away for years and feels that this is the time to reveal it again to some 'Good Oppos' having a beer with him in the sergeants' mess bar.

Maybe a new 'Dit' is formed, such as Neil (the ex-armourer and therefore expert with all small arms) making the observation to a currently serving Royal Marine who was on hand to talk about the modern grenade launchers and laser sights on show to these 'Old Soldiers' in a display tent at Bickliegh Barracks in 2017.

Neil bent down and picked up an 84mm anti-tank gun from a side table. 'Gosh, are they still using the 84 mm in Afghan? We used that in the Falklands.'

'No, fuck off mate, we picked that up this morning from the Corps museum at RM Poole,' came the slightly less than respectful reply from the smartly turned-out, wide-shouldered youth wearing the Green Beret and Commando flashes as the rest of the tent joined in the chortles of laughter.

The legends still have a part to play too. True to form, the Bickleigh 'Cloud' normally forms up on the edge of the parade ground whenever three ranks form up for an event. 2017 was no exception. General Vaux, our CO from the Falklands – now in his 70s – together with the most senior command team of the Royal Marines of the Falkland era (mostly in their 80s), was given the responsibility of the decision, quietly and respectfully, by the current CO of 42 Commando, for having the parade outside on the parade ground in the rain, and maybe risk pneumonia amongst half the gathering of veterans, or inside in the warm and dry gym.

'Well, we've all been a bit wet before, so let's go out onto the parade ground!' General Vaux announced to all on the microphone, to a titter of laughter that ran around the gym.

REMEMBER THEM

T hese days I find myself in the fortunate position of spending much of my time sailing around Northern Europe with family and friends on my own yacht. I was hugely inspired by my time in the Corps, and especially my time on the Corps yacht and at the Joint Services Sailing Centre in the 1980s. When I retired from my second career after twenty-three years as an Inspector in the Suffolk Constabulary, I decided that I would start a third career and do something I enjoyed but didn't have to do as I was told all the time. It would also be nice if I could also get paid for doing it, so I became a RYA Yachtmaster Instructor and eventually a RYA Examiner.

Upon approaching the Scheldt Estuary in Holland after a North Sea crossing, not only do my crew get a thorough navigational brief of this busy entrance into the Dutch inland waterways, but I also point out on the port side Walcheren Island, where, in November 1944, Royal Marines from 41, 47 and 48 Commando landed as part of Operation *Infatuate* to assault and take out the heavy German naval guns protecting the entrance to the Scheldt and the strategic port of Antwerp.

Once on a poor weather day when we were stuck in Breskins, two of the crew and I hired some bikes and made a cycling pilgrimage to Westkapple on Walcheren and the memorial to the 103 killed in action from 4 Commando Brigade. It's very touching to see how well the memorials are looked after. Each year on the anniversary of the liberation of the town of Westkapple, a local child is assigned a name and takes flowers to each of the graves of the young Royal Marines.

In 2016, after a beam reach sail (i.e., a fast and fairly easy point of sail that makes good ground straight to your destination) across the English Channel to Normandy, we entered Caen Canal in France and

I pointed out the route taken by 45 Commando as they made their way inland to Pegasus Bridge from Sword Beach on D-Day. The fallen from this day of days are recorded all over the beaches in that part of France. Many white crosses are immaculately kept in pristine garden military cemeteries dotted around just inland of the beaches.

When exiting the Solent going west, I usually stop in the unique Poole Harbour and show the crew the most excellent pubs on the quayside. For those who are interested, I will guide them on the short walk through the town to the memorial of the landing craft crew of *Foxtrot 4*, bombed whilst moving the Guards to Bluff Cove in 1982. My good oppo Jim was on board and survived, but all his crew were killed or wounded. Marine 'Griff' Griffin is cast on that bronze plaque, together with the other crew members of *Foxtrot 4*, and I run my hand over the cold bronze each time I visit.

A twelve-sided bandstand sits in a prominent position on Deal seafront in Kent, a memorial to the eleven Royal Marines murdered by the IRA in 1989. This one takes me some time to trace each name with my index finger, as they were all people who I had seen laughing, joking and enjoying being alive with their whole lives in front of them.

Memorials to young men and women are dotted around every battlefield in the world and every service town and most parishes in the UK.

There is one on Plymouth Hoe that I only found a couple of years ago when I was about to sail for the Channel Islands the following day. I decided to go for a walk on the Hoe instead of having beer on board, as we had an early tide to catch the next morning and fresh air was better than a fuzzy head. I walked down the steps to Belvedere Memorial Garden, overlooking Plymouth Sound, and came upon a neat memorial to all the British servicemen who had been killed in the 1982 Falklands conflict. There, third down, under Royal Marines was

'Mne C Davison'

This inscription was for Lance Corporal PO37269B Colin 'George' Davison, who died aged only 21. I traced my friend's name with my index finger on the stainless steel plaque.